BFI FILM CLASSICS

. . . .

Edward Buscombe

SERIES EDITOR

Cinema is a fragile medium. Many of the great classic films of the past now exist, if at all, in damaged or incomplete prints. Concerned about the deterioration in the physical state of our film heritage, the National Film and Television Archive, a Division of the British Film Institute, has compiled a list of 360 key films in the history of the cinema. The long-term goal of the Archive is to build a collection of perfect show-prints of these films, which will then be screened regularly at the Museum of the Moving Image in London in a year-round repertory.

BFI Film Classics is a series of books commissioned to stand alongside these titles. Authors, including film critics and scholars, film-makers, novelists, historians and those distinguished in the arts, have been invited to write on a film of their choice, drawn from the Archive's list. Each volume presents the author's own insights into the chosen film, together with a brief production history and a detailed filmography, notes and bibliography. The numerous illustrations have been specially made from the Archive's own prints.

Could scarcely be improved upon ... informative, intelligent, jargon-free companions
The Observer

... each manages to give a sense of the film in question as it unfolds, without falling back on tedious explanations. The background information is finely researched and gracefully communicated.
The Times Saturday Review

The BFI's excellent new Film Classics series
Literary Review

Cannily but elegantly packaged BFI Classics will make for a neat addition to the most discerning shelves
New Statesman & Society

Oh, No It Isn't the Moon—
IT'S NOSE IN BLOOM!

...And a nose-gay to you, Mr. Fields
for another uproarious comedy jammed
with uncontrollable laughter...on your
3,000-smile joy ride to buy an orange
grove that turns out to be a lemon!
You wrecked us, Mr. Fields . . . but it's
swell to be wrecked by a guy like you!

Adolph Zukor presents

W. C. Fields

in "IT'S A GIFT"

with Baby LeRoy

Directed by Norman McLeod • A Paramount Picture

THEATRE

BFI FILM

CLASSICS

IT'S A GIFT

· · · · · · · · · · · · · · · · · · · ·

Simon Louvish

BFI PUBLISHING

First published in 1994 by the
BRITISH FILM INSTITUTE
21 Stephen Street, London W1P 1PL

The British Film Institute exists
to encourage the development of film, television
and video in the United Kingdom,
and to promote knowledge, understanding and
enjoyment of the culture of the moving image.
Its activities include the National Film and
Television Archive; the National Film Theatre;
the Museum of the Moving Image;
the London Film Festival; the production and
distribution of film and video; funding and support for
regional activities; Library and Information Services;
Stills, Posters and Designs; Research;
Publishing and Education; and the monthly
Sight and Sound magazine.

British Library Cataloguing-in-Publication Data
A catalogue record for this book is available from the British Library

ISBN 0–85170–472–7

Designed by
Andrew Barron & Collis Clements Associates

Typesetting by
Fakenham Photosetting Limited, Norfolk

Printed in Great Britain by
The Trinity Press, Worcester

CONTENTS

....

In Memoriam

Kate Felton-Fields,
Harriet Hughes-Fields,
Joseph Patrick McEvoy

'Out of the cradle, endlessly rocking . . .'

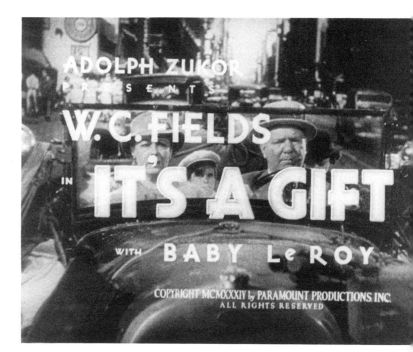

1

....

'SUFFERIN' SCIATICA!'

SYNOPSIS: Harold Bissonette owns a small-town grocery store in New Jersey, running the daily gauntlet of his nagging wife, demanding daughter, loud-mouthed small son, prudish townspeople, blind or just plain ornery customers, rapacious salesmen and, of course, Baby LeRoy. But his dream to up stakes and run an orange farm in California is made possible by the death of a rich relative, Uncle Bean. To the horror of his wife and the tears of his daughter, Mr Bissonette (pronounced Bissonay) sells the grocery store and drags his family in a battered jalopy westwards across the continent. The orange ranch is not what it seemed in the brochure, but Harold Bissonette triumphs in time for the final credits to roll.

THE CRITICS RAVE: 'It is about time that the Fields enthusiasts got together and demanded that their hero have a production worthy of him. *It's a Gift* looks as though it had taken two days to make, had cost $100, and had been photographed with one of the early Biograph cameras.

It is clumsy, crude and quite amateurish in its appearance. It merely happens that a great comedian appears in it and has a free hand in his brilliant clowning, with the result that the defects become unimportant, and the film emerges as a comedy delight. Just for a change, though, a skillful production might be accorded Mr Fields, just to see what the effect would be.'   'Argus', *The Literary Digest*, 1935

....

Over a back-projection of urban-Hollywood streets, a battered 1930s motor car springs into view, bearing the archetypal American family: Pop and Mom, bickering in the front seat, while daughter and small boy fret in the back. The soundtrack wells up in that crackling 'Noiseless Western Electric' recording of 'California Here We Come'. The titles rack forward on the screen. Those familiar names, that long gone age: ADOLPH ZUKOR, W. C. FIELDS, BABY LEROY. Directed by NORMAN MCLEOD. Produced by WILLIAM LEBARON. The backdrop changes to a country road. The sequence fades.

We have entered a country that has become part of our dreams. The land of the 'nefilim': the giants before a more mundane creation gave us the pigmies of the cathode-ray tube. In our day they too have become pigmies, trapped in the cycle of rescheduled repeats on 'terrestrial' and 'extra-terrestrial' venues. Technology can now flesh out their spectral black and white to a pasty delirium of colours, and soon will be able to give us the powers to alter the very fabric of the dream itself, to rewrite plots, to change the endings. The clowns themselves will not have the last laugh. . .

But let's pretend that we have walked back into the past, not to change it to fit our impoverished conceits, but to experience it in all its fading glory. The picture fades in to show the postman walking up to the front of an old three-storeyed apartment house in a suburban street. He extracts a letter: to Harold Bissonette, 27 Clint Avenue, Wappinger Falls, New Jersey. No matter that there is not a Wappinger Falls in New Jersey, though there is one in New York state. But the right name is more important here than mere geographical accuracy, as we will find out.

We cut to the interior of this home. A small boy is rushing about on his skates. Mom, an archetypally austere figure, reads the letter, which is from Aunt Matilda: 'Uncle Bean has been in very bad health for weeks. We're all afraid he will never get up again.'

The small boy babbles breathlessly: 'If Uncle Bean dies, Pop says he'll buy an orange ranch and we'll go off to California to live.'

'Your father says a lot of things,' says Mom.

The young, prim daughter is upset. She rattles the bathroom door: 'Pop, hurry up, I want to come in.'

'Come in, I'm only shavin',' comes that grating drawl, in reply.

The scene is set for the first of many titanic struggles between Harold Bissonette and the universe. The apparently mundane setting of the bathroom is an arena full of pitfalls and obstacles. There will be a battle of wills between father and daughter, between male and female, between Man and a variety of uncontrollable objects: bathroom cabinets, hair brushes, mirrors, chairs. There is mortal danger. A cut-throat razor in the hand versus a faceful of lather, to be tamed at all costs.

The closing and opening of the bathroom cabinet mirror leave the

'Mortal danger': Harold tries to shave

shaving man frozen in place, razor dangerously poised. He moves behind his daughter to face the mirror's new location, as she brushes her hair, only to receive a wad of hair in the mouth. Giving up and moving across the bathroom to try to shave in the reflection from a tin can, he is stopped in his tracks by her gargling.

HAROLD: You want me to cut my throat, keep that up.
She gargles on.
HAROLD (mumbling): You evidently do ...

The wavy image in the can almost makes him cut his ear off. He fixes a small round mirror to the ceiling and tries to follow it as it revolves, swinging savagely at his throat as it comes round. No use. He tries sitting on the back of the bathroom chair to raise himself to the mirror, but falls down into it. Finally he tries shaving while lying on his back on the chair. His daughter, Mildred, leaves, just as the little boy, Norman, followed by Mom, rushes in to find him in this bizarre posture.

MRS BISSONETTE: What kind of tomfoolery are you up to now?
HAROLD BISSONETTE: Ah'm shaving ...
MRS BISSONETTE: Well, why don't you shave over there? (Points to perfectly available bathroom cabinet.)
HAROLD: What ...? Oh ... Uh ...
MRS BISSONETTE: Of all the drivelling idiots! Hurry up and come to breakfast!

Hastening to obey, and sticking a flower in his buttonhole – 'Beautiful morning, isn't it?' – Mr Bissonette trips on his son's skate and achieves a perfect pratfall into the dining room.

HAROLD: Sufferin' sciatica!

But the clown's bad day has only begun ...

2

....

'HAVE YOU HAD THIS TOOTH PULLED BEFORE?'

It's a Gift was Fields's sixteenth sound film, and his fifth in 1934 alone. It was his most prolific year, which saw at least one more masterpiece – *The Old-Fashioned Way* – as well as two vintage works: *Six of a Kind* and *You're Telling Me*, and the rather less lustrous *Mrs Wiggs of the Cabbage Patch*, which teamed the clown with Zasu Pitts. This latter experience appears to be referred to in a throwaway line in 1941's *Never Give a Sucker an Even Break* when Fields asks his starlet niece, Gloria Jean: 'Do you want to grow up and be dumb, like Zasu Pitts?' A small example of the clown's prodigious grudges.

As with most screen comedians, the same credits keep cropping up, in crew and cast. All the 1934 films were produced by William LeBaron. Both *It's a Gift* and *The Old-Fashioned Way* had a screenplay by Jack Cunningham based on a story by one Charles Bogle (a more mundane Fields alias than the later Mahatma Kane Jeeves, or Otis Criblecoblis). The squat figure of Tammany Young is present in three of the year's pictures as Fields's sidekick-cum-doormat. Baby LeRoy turns up in two of them, and Fields's most potent straight-woman, Kathleen Howard, provides the chilling wind of reality in *You're Telling Me* and *It's a Gift*. In 1935 she was to reprise her role as the most nagging wife in movie history in *The Man on the Flying Trapeze*.

The credits of 1934 display different directors, as if one round with Fields necessitated a good rest before the next gruelling bout. Leo McCarey, Earle Kenton, William Beaudine and Norman Taurog all took their turn through the year. *It's a Gift* was directed by Norman McLeod, who had directed Fields in his cameo as Humpty Dumpty in *Alice in Wonderland* (1933), and had already slugged it out with the Marx Brothers in *Monkey Business* and *Horse Feathers* (1931 and 1932). McLeod had served as a pilot with the Royal Canadian Air Force in the First World War, and had begun his film career as an animator in 1919, a combination which may have served him ideally in dealing with erratic comedians. After Fields, he directed two of the *Topper* movies and went on to steer such later talents as Danny Kaye in *The Kid from Brooklyn* and *The Secret Life of Walter Mitty*, and Bob Hope in *The Paleface* and *My Favourite Spy*.

Fields's next film after *It's a Gift* was *David Copperfield*, in which he achieved a long cherished ambition when he was cast as Mr Micawber. Under George Cukor's direction, and playing a classic, Fields was somewhat tamed, but only Dickens's woeful failure to provide the necessary scene in the original material prevented him from performing his poolroom sketch. The centrality of Mr Micawber to Fields's oeuvre, however, should not be underestimated.

After *It's a Gift* and *David Copperfield* Fields played in twelve more films. In all Fields appeared in thirty-nine films, eleven of them silent, though most of the silent films have remained unavailable for many years. And this prolific film career was a second vocation after more than two decades on the stage.

Of all the great movie clowns Fields is the one whose life and screen image are most intertwined. His own chosen biography comes closest to the idea expressed in John Ford's *The Man Who Shot Liberty Valance* – 'When the legend becomes fact, print the legend.' Fields's primary biographer, Robert Lewis Taylor, in *W. C. Fields – His Follies and Fortunes* (1948), did just that, providing a dynamic and ribald account culled largely from the clown's own tales. This version was unchallenged until Fields's grandson, Ronald J. Fields, attempted to correct the myth in *W. C. Fields By Himself* (1974), a book consisting mostly of a treasure trove of previously unknown Fields letters, unpublished treatments, and fragments of scripts.

In the case of Fields, fiction is much stranger than fact: the grand myth of a Dickensian childhood, his escape from the angry fists of his father, James Dukinfield, to a bleak life in the streets of Philadelphia in 1890, aged 11, reduced to stealing food. But even Fields himself, while relishing the myth, could slip into nostalgia about those times: 'The trolley-car parties or trolley rides took the place of the old hayrides in the summertime,' he related to his friend Gene Fowler. 'A party would get together, engage an open trolley car, and adorn it with bunting. Noise ran rampant; the occupants would blow horns and make noises with rattles, and the smart alecks would make cracks at the ghillies who stood on the corners or who passed with their girls' (Taylor, p. 15).

'Nautch' joints, 25 cents for a knee trembler in Middie Alley, band concerts and cinnamon buns. It hardly sounds like the dark satanic mills. 'I'd like to see Paris before I die!' Fields calls out as he is about to be hanged in *My Little Chickadee* (1940), adding as the rope tugs: 'Settle for Philadelphia!'

A city, Taylor tells us, of 'high moral indignation and average morals'. It was, according to Fields, 'the greatest cemetery in the world … Great town for breweries … all had saloons in conjunction … owned and operated them that way … Gilmore and Sousa were the bands that played in Willow Grove Park.' His reminiscences of his home life were also oddly poignant: 'Everybody sat in the kitchen in the wintertime. It was so God-damned cold in the rest of the house you couldn't stand it. The kitchen was the only place with any heat. We used to make snowballs, dip them in some kind of flavouring, and have a party … One year we had a blizzard there, a big one. It went over the horses' heads.'

One can hear the timbre of a typical Fields monologue, that mixture of warped memory and fantasy, the surreal crossing of lines. Like the mad contours of his two-reel short, *The Fatal Glass of Beer* (1932), with its ridiculous posture at the Arctic shack's door – 'and it ain't a fit night out for man nor beast!' as he is hit in the face by a flurry of fake snow.

At the start of his career, William Claude Dukinfield invented a character called W. C. Fields, and then immersed himself in his creation. The legendary Fields had to be an outsider, a kicker against the pricks of society. The fictional Fields became a prominent Philadelphia juvenile offender, a self-made Artful Dodger. In later years, Fields would say, in one of his many bons mots: 'Never having had the time to attend school, I never studied long enough to find education boring.' But this was, typically, a lie which told the truth. The boy yearned, by all accounts, for a non-conforming life, and he found his purpose in show business.

In fact, his grandson tells us, the Dukinfield family were not poor. James Dukinfield was not, he claims, a vendor of fruit and veg from a cart but a 'commission merchant' dealing in those commodities. He was a strict and somewhat unhumorous man, but there was, it appears, no major family trauma that led to William Claude leaving home. His mother packed him a couple of sandwiches in a paper bag and walked with him to the trolley bus which took him to his first tour, with the Keith Circuit, in 1899, when he was 19 years old. He left town, not on the run from the police, but merely bitten by the bug of vaudeville.

He was a fan who turned into a pro. Legend has him honing his skills at the pool table in a bar his father owned, then taking a job racking balls at a poolhall. And so W. C. Fields was born. But poolroom routines, like juggling, were a staple of vaudeville, a particularly famous one being a duo, Weber and Field, a coincidence of name that I am sure William Claude would not have overlooked.

In his first film, *Pool Sharks* in 1915, Fields reprised his famous skill at the pool table. The pool-shark, the man who pretends to be a dunce until he moves in to fleece the sucker, was one of the first building blocks of the clown to be. But the act itself, as Fields performed it on stage in the first decade of the twentieth century, had to wait twenty more years before being revealed authentically on the screen, in 1934. In *Six of a Kind*, directed by Leo McCarey, he plays a Nevada Sheriff, 'Honest John', who proceeds to a melange of tricks at the pool table, with a selection of twisted cues and the familiar non-stop patter, finally sticking his cue right into the table without potting a single ball.

In 1890s Philadelphia, Fields sneaked into the Keith Vaudeville Theatre to watch the famous Burns Brothers juggle. Trying out the trick with apples and oranges, he soon discovered a natural aptitude for juggling, the skill which was to be his first vehicle for a stardom beyond his wildest dreams.

Or was it? The successful performers, like politicians or the self-made capitalists of nineteenth-century America, had to be ruthlessly single-minded. This single-mindedness, as we shall see, extracted a high price from Fields, but created a unique persona. The legend presents us with a young man desperate to escape the trap of poverty and a scarred childhood, just as another young genius, Charlie Chaplin, escaped from Victorian London and the Lambeth workhouse. But whatever the motive, the driving force was prodigious, as Fields was propelled by his vital ambition into his first highly vulnerable engagements with amusement parks and travelling burlesque shows.

Fields's second film of 1934, *The Old-Fashioned Way* (itself a remake of the vanished silent, *Two Flaming Youths*, 1927), was his fond attempt at recasting those days. As the Great McGonigle, Fields steers his seedy nineteenth-century travelling company from town to town, one jump ahead of the law and boarding house landladies unreasonably demanding payment. It includes the definitive pastiche of old-style lowbrow melodrama with its sentimental play within the film – 'The Drunkard' – and a unique reprise of Fields's juggling act with cigar boxes, according to Taylor his very first trick. The miraculous skill with which the apparently clumsy performer keeps the boxes poised in mid-air opens a chink in the curtain of time behind which Fields's unfilmed career as the world's greatest juggler can be all too briefly glimpsed. The film also includes the most useful scene of how to get out of a boarding house without paying, when Fields, caught in the act of trying to sneak out with his luggage, pretends to be taking in the trunk of a colleague who, he says, has just arrived to join him in his quarters.

'No, you don't!' insists the landlady, Mrs Wendleschaeffer, 'I've had enough of your kind! Take that trunk right out of here!'

'Very well,' Fields mumbles, hurrying his stooge, Tammany Young, down the stairs and out of the front door, 'but you'll regret this in the morning.'

3
. . . .
'GRUBBING, GRUBBING, GRUBBING . . .'

Fields's most legendary early engagement was with Fortescue's Pier, a seaside amusement show. As well as juggling, he was required to swim out several times a day beyond the pier and pretend to drown. When the lifeguards fished him out, the crowd which gathered would remain to see the shows and eat at Fortescue's beer garden and restaurant. This added to Fields's list of paranoias an absolute loathing of swimming. In fact it must have been those early days at the lower end of show business, rather than boyhood escapades, which most scarred the young clown's soul, providing him with his fear of failure well into his age of success, and with another building block of his myth, the obsessive opening of secret bank accounts in every town and city he passed. Alas, Will Fowler, son of his old friend Gene, unforgivably quashed this fine tale in an interview, claiming that Fields had a mere twenty-one bank accounts, quite prudently, in different cities, all under his own name.

A series of breaks in New York, beginning at the Globe Museum – which engaged him, he claimed, when the headless lady fractured her skull – led him swiftly up the ladder of success in vaudeville, until he was earning the princely sum of $125 a week. Booked through the William Morris Agency, he travelled coast to coast, earning more money and constantly honing his act.

By 1901 he was famous enough to be offered his first foreign tour, to Europe. At the Palace in London he was billed as 'Wm. C. Fields, the Distinguished Comedian and Greatest Juggler on Earth, Eccentric Tramp'. Edward, Prince of Wales, never a man to miss out on a new show, famously attended his performance. By his own dubious accounts, Fields was rowdy in pubs and attracted the attention of policemen in London, Paris and Berlin. He used to wax eloquent about the comparisons between different jails and their cuisines, real or imagined. But in England it was not only the beer he discovered, but English writing too.

Taylor prints the legend: Fields repairs in a hansom cab to a second-hand bookseller with an empty trunk. 'Fill the trunk with books!' he demands. 'Does the gentleman favour any particular colour? Volumes as will set well in a trunk – records of incoming and outgoing vessels, together with tonnage, since 1832 . . .' 'There seems to be some misapprehension,' says Fields, 'I want the best books you've got, the finest authors in English literature' (Taylor, pp. 82–3).

Shakespeare, Sir Thomas More, Milton, Chaucer. And additional volumes of Dickens, whom he had discovered in his teens, at the same time that, according to his legend, he was neglecting his education. He was influenced, too, by a fellow vaudevillian, one Owen McGiveney, who specialised in Dickens characters. Mr Micawber was a frequent voice.

It is salutary to trace Fields's language, as it twists and weaves through his films, to the first appearance of Micawber in *David Copperfield*, the role that destiny (and David O. Selznick) was to put in Fields's way:

'This is Mr Micawber,' said Mr Quinion to me . . .
    I made him a bow.
    'Under the impression,' said Mr Micawber, 'that your

peregrinations in this metropolis have not as yet been extensive,
and that you might have some difficulty in penetrating the arcana
of the Modern Babylon in the direction of the City Road, in
short,' said Mr Micawber, in another burst of confidence, 'that you
might lose yourself – I shall be happy to call this evening, and
install you in the knowledge of the nearest way.'

I thanked him with all my heart, for it was friendly in him to
offer to take that trouble.

'At what hour,' said Mr Micawber, 'shall I –'

'At about eight,' said Mr Quinion.

'At about eight,' said Mr Micawber. 'I beg to wish you good
day, Mr Quinion. I will intrude no longer.'

So he put on his hat, and went out with his cane under his
arm: very upright, and humming a tune when he was clear of the
counting-house.

One need only add that rasping, Mid-west drawl to hear the creative
voice of Charles Bogle, Otis Criblecoblis, and Mahatma Kane Jeeves.
Micawber, generous, hapless, debt and family-ridden, became another
central building block of the character that blossomed into life when the
boon of sound was added to the silent pool-shark and putative man
about town. The self-identification of Fields with the boy heroes of
Dickens – David Copperfield, Oliver Twist, Pip of *Great Expectations* –
clearly fuelled his subsequent rewriting of his own childhood: life, once
again, imitates art.

Returning from his European tours, Fields pursued a gruelling
schedule of work, appearing in his first play, *The Ham Tree*, and
performing in two shows a night for two different companies. The
outbreak of war in 1914 found him in Australia, from where he sailed to
San Francisco. Back in New York, he was spotted by an assistant to the
great Ziegfeld, who signed him for the Ziegfeld Follies of 1915. Louise
Brooks, who met him in the Follies and was to be his co-star in *It's the
Old Army Game* (1926), gave an insight into the stage Fields:

I have never loved and laughed at W. C. Fields in films as I loved
and laughed at him in the theatre. . . In the theatre, he was a
make-believe character playing in a make-believe world. In films,

he was a real character acting in real stories. On the stage, the crafty idiocy with which he attempted to extricate himself from ludicrous situations was unbelievably funny. The same idiocy attending the same situations on screen gave his 'real' character a degraded quality, often a cruel and destructive one ...

My second reason for preferring Fields on stage ... is that on the stage the audience saw all of him all the time ... [On the film set of *Sally of the Sawdust*] he paid no attention to camera setups. For each shot, he would rehearse the same business to exasperating perfection while his co-star, Carole Dempster, and the Director D. W. Griffith sat bored and limp in chairs beside the camera. Long shot, medium shot, two-shot or close-up, Bill performed as if he were standing whole before an audience that could appreciate every detail of his costume and follow the dainty disposition of his hands and feet. Every time the camera drew closer, it cut off another piece of him and deprived him of some comic effect... As he ignored camera setups, he ignored the cutting room, and could only curse the finished film, seeing his timing ruined by haphazard cuts. (Louise Brooks, 1982.)

It was in this period (1915–25) that Fields developed the routines which were to be honed and reprised in his films. The basic fact to be known about Fields's movies is this: although he appeared in a variety of silent and sound features, in different roles, following various scripts, he always tried, whenever he had the opportunity to insert his own scenes or write his own scripts, to recapture on film the original sketches which were the basis of his stage success. Thus 'The Drug Store' became a segment of *It's the Old Army Game* and *The Pharmacist*. 'The Picnic' found its way into *It's the Old Army Game* and *It's a Gift*. 'At the Dentist's' became *The Dentist* for Mack Sennett. 'Stolen Bonds' became *The Fatal Glass of Beer*. 'A Joy Ride' found its way into *It's a Gift*. 'An Episode on the Links' became *The Golf Specialist*. And 'The Back Porch' was reprised in *It's the Old Army Game* and later in the famous scene in *It's a Gift*. The metamorphoses through which some of these sketches went give us a fascinating insight into the clown's art, as I shall attempt to show.

Fields appeared in the Ziegfeld Follies every year until 1921, but his next step towards the character he was to portray in movies came in 1923 with his first overwhelming success in a play, the musical comedy *Poppy* by Dorothy Donnelly. His role as Eustace McGargle, a fairground rogue who brought up an orphaned girl, was acclaimed by both critics and audiences. This led to his first proper movie part, as a drunken British sergeant in a period picture, *Janice Meredith*. But *Poppy* itself was bought for the screen by Paramount Pictures, which hired D. W. Griffith to direct it, as *Sally of the Sawdust*, in 1925.

Sally of the Sawdust, a mint print of which survives in the Museum of Modern Art in New York, reveals itself to be, paradoxically but not surprisingly, the best directed of Fields's films. In its tale of the redemption of an old rich couple who discover that the crass showman's adopted girl is in fact their unknown grandchild, it is clearly more Griffith than Fields. Fields gets in a wonderful intertitle put-down of the stern old judge who, unwittingly, is planning to send his own offspring to jail: 'He has a face that looks like its worn out four bodies.' His portrayal of McGargle, the travelling rascal with a golden heart, provides another building block of the clown.

The Dentist

Fields made a second film with Griffith, *That Royle Girl*, which is listed as missing, and was judged a failure by the critics. But it was Fields's following film, *It's the Old Army Game*, which first established on screen the other part of the Fields persona – the small-town druggist or grocer, with his succession of mad business schemes.

4
....

'A GAME OF SKILL WHERE THE HAND DECEIVES THE EYE!'

As *It's the Old Army Game* (1926) is the original template of *It's a Gift*, its well worth taking a look at the silent film version. The film opens with a long title:

> This is the epic of the American druggist – a community benefactor. His shop is at once the social center, the place of countless conveniences and the forum of public thought. It is the druggist we seek in hours of suffering and adversity, and day and night he is oft the agency between life and death . . .

A car shoots across the countryside at speed, cutting dangerously ahead of a rushing train, to stop at the house of the local druggist, Elmer Prettywillie, 'apothecary and humanitarian'. The driver is Elise Cavanna, the languid and angular comedienne who was to be Fields's foil and wife in three of his later Mack Sennett shorts. She has awoken the druggist to call for a two cent stamp, but rushes out without paying. Searching for a mailbox she sets off the fire alarm by mistake, bringing the fire brigade to poke about Elmer's store and cash box in the vain hope of finding a fire.

The Prettywillie menage includes a nagging sister, an obnoxious small boy, Mickey – 'a combination of Peck's Bad Boy, Gyp the Blood and Jesse James', and a counter assistant, Marilyn, the peerless Louise Brooks.

Fire breaks out in a cigar box after the firemen leave, but Elmer manages to put it out. This dumb-play Fields is more spry than we're used to, his springy walk owing a debt of sorts to Chaplin, though he might banish the thought. He wears a snub moustache, which was only to come off after his first three sound movies. There are still echoes of the circus showman in this small-town chemist situated somewhere in Florida. Having chased the firemen away from Louise Brooks, Elmer settles down in a hammock on his porch for some rest. But he has little chance. A woman brings out a suspiciously large crying baby. Elmer tries to stuff a sheet in its mouth. The baby pushes it out. Elmer hands it a mirror and a mallet but the child wallops him over the head. He leaps up, breaking the railing over the second-floor landing, and is dangling the child over the edge maliciously when mother returns to save her tot. Much ado with an immense safety pin follows, and attempts by Elmer to manoeuvre baby into its pram with his boot clamped down on its hand. After being beaned with a milk bottle Elmer gives up, a title saying, as he walks away: 'Uncle will give you some nice razor blades to play with.'

The next interruption is from a vegetable vendor. Elmer rushes indoors and comes out with a rifle, but the vendor has gone. The scissors-grinder is next ('Scissors to GRIND!'), then the ice man, who leaves him a slippery block. Much fiddling with block of ice and ice box whose lid keeps closing. Finally Elmer throws the ice in the trash can and returns to his hammock, only to knock down the rifle, which goes off, bringing the hammock down.

The 'porch' sketch, along with the 'drug-store' sketch and the 'picnic' sketch, are three Fields's stage pieces reprised in *It's the Old Army Game*. The original porch scene, as performed on the stage, included the following interruptions:

> A newsboy with squeaky shoes going up and down the stairs.
>
> A woman yelling across to neighbours that there is a phone call for them in the drugstore.
>
> A ringing alarm clock.
>
> A baby – Fields's own kid in the stage skit – crying so that Papa stuffs sheets in its mouth. Baby hits Papa with mallet.
>
> A fruit and veg peddler crying his wares.
>
> Collapse of the hammock.
>
> A scissors-grinder.
>
> An exploding gun.

> A policeman's motorcycle backfires.
>
> The iceman: Fields rushes to take in the block of ice, can't get it in the ice box, finally throws it in the trash can.

This has clearly been faithfully followed in the silent film, though the sketch, as we shall see, will be completely recast in *It's a Gift*.

In the picnic sketch, also reprised in the silent film, Fields and his family, on a day out, drive onto the grounds of a palatial mansion, trashing the lawn with their paper wrappings and breaking in to the house to find some plates, outraged at the idea that the owner might lock his door against an 'honest American tax-payer'.

In the original 'Drug Store', Fields is plagued by browsers who come into his store without buying, asking to have a speck removed from their eye, to use the bathroom, or buy a stamp just to get a free gift. All three sketches, along with 'A Joy Ride', originated in a musical revue, *The Comic Supplement of American Life*, co-written with Fields by veteran revue writer Joseph Patrick McEvoy.

It's the Old Army Game

J. P. McEvoy is the elusive 'from a story by' credit in *It's the Old Army Game* and *It's a Gift*, alongside the screenwriters Tom J. Geraghty for the earlier film and Jack Cunningham for the later. *The Comic Supplement* was conceived as a kind of cartoon-strip revue of current American life, as a special show for Florenz Ziegfeld to complement the *Ziegfeld Follies of 1924*. The cast included Betty Compton, Ray Dooley and Fields, and the show featured such forgotten songs (composed by Henry Souvaine and Con Conrad) as 'American Prelude', 'Cafeteria Chow', 'The Cop and the Nurse', 'Goo Goo Goo', 'Jungle Joy', 'Little Two by Four', the 'Scrubwomen's Ballet' and 'Sunday Poipers', whatever they were. Not surprisingly perhaps, the show flopped on tour after three weeks in Newark and Washington and never opened in New York. But Ziegfeld liked the sketches, and added them to the Ziegfeld Follies proper in a special '1925 Latest Edition', which became a roaring success.

It is impossible to know how much is Fields and how much McEvoy in the original writing of the sketches. Clearly Fields felt a sufficient debt to credit McEvoy in both films. This has to be significant, since Fields's motto was 'never steal, except from other comedians', and he actually patented his own original sketches, such as his golf skit, listed as 'Copyright Number 109' on 4 November 1918.

McEvoy, who wrote for numerous Broadway revues, had also written two novels on show business, which were later filmed as *Show Girl* and *Show Girl in Hollywood* (1928 and 1930). In the 1930s, he co-scripted material for George Burns and Gracie Allen, Jack Benny and Shirley Temple. His greatest success, for all that, was his 1923 play *The Potters*, which in 1927 became Fields's third movie.

In *The Potters*, Fields plays an oppressed family man who invests the family savings in an oil speculation. His wife, Ma Potter, is opposed to this project, and the two spar on from scene to scene. There is a young daughter with a fiancé Fields can't abide. In the end the oil speculation turns out a bonanza and Pa Potter triumphs against the odds. Like many of Fields's silents, *The Potters* has remained unseen for decades. But we can perceive in the synopsis several important building blocks that will make up the Bissonette home.

The oil scam of *The Potters* is anticipated by the fraudulent lots Elmer Prettywillie is conned into selling in *It's the Old Army Game*. This provides the love interest in the picture, with fugitive salesman William Gaxton falling for Louise Brooks. Elmer's involvement precipitates his near downfall, with the angry townspeople closing in on him en masse as he runs off, alone, down the street. But unknown to him the lots are valuable after all, and all is saved at the end.

It's the Old Army Game reveals all the drawbacks which impeded Fields's march to silent stardom. The film was directed by Eddie Sutherland, a comedy specialist, and maintains a good flow of gags and action. But it is clear that the porch scene creaks under the burden of trying to get round the lack of sound, and Fields himself later called it 'awful', claiming that he had no say in the way it was filmed. Certainly the exclusively visual comedy Fields was reduced to, despite the critics' acknowledgment of his 'pantomimist's skill', could not match the work being done at the same time by Chaplin, Keaton, Langdon and Lloyd.

The vital missing ingredient, the Voice, beloved of stage fans, had yet to be unveiled for a movie audience. But these Fields silent films displayed for the first time on the screen another staple of the comedian's world: those harrowing, harridan women.

5

. . . .

'THOSE WERE MY MOTHER'S FEATHERS!'

Like Mr Micawber, Harold Bissonette of Wappinger Falls, New Jersey, is blessed, or cursed, with a family for whom he cannot quite provide. Not, at any rate, in terms of their own dreams, desires or great expectations. Fields's women fall into three strict categories: shrews, spoiled brats and sweet young things. In *It's a Gift*, the daughter, haughty and temperamental in turns, is played by Jean Rouverol, and Bissonette's wife by Kathleen Howard.

An unnerving photograph of Fields's mother displays a face remarkably similar to the clown himself in middle age. It was she who was the source of those mumbled asides, commenting on all and sundry as she used to sit on the porch and greet the neighbours, murmuring out of the side of her mouth what she really thought of them.

Fields told all sorts of tall tales about his parents, veering between claims that his father and mother had both suffered from leprosy to co-opting them into show business to prove that 'I've got the theatre in my blood.' Mrs Dukinfield, formerly Kate Felton, was a native Philadelphian, but his father, James Dukinfield, was an English immigrant who had felt so passionately for his adopted country that he had fought in the Civil War for the Union. Both mother and children used to enjoy needling him for his apparent lack of humour.

At the age of 21, in 1900, Fields married Harriet Hughes of 423 West 25th Street, New York, and thereby all the trouble starts. At first she helped him out with his act, as a 'Tramp's Assistant'; an early photograph shows him rounding on her in fake anger after a dropped ball. But she was pregnant while he was on tour abroad and he was absent at the birth of W. C. Fields Junior, always referred to later as Claude (he was to become a well-liked lawyer). Hattie stayed in the United States with the child, while the clown pursued his career abroad. Photographs of the period reveal Fields as a brash and determined young man who would not be deflected from his path. Hattie, Ronald Fields told an interviewer, would have liked Fields to give up his wandering life and be a proper father. Although in the first few years of the marriage this conflict was restrained, it gradually turned into a virulent war, with Fields accusing Hattie of poisoning his son's mind against him. There is no longer any doubt that all those shrewish, nagging wives rampaging through Fields's stage acts and later films derive from his deep sense of injury and revenge, as his letters to his wife, published by his grandson, confirm. 'For ten years,' he writes in 1915, 'you have inculcated into the boy's mind stories of my atrocities, you used every artifice and cunning you could employ to turn him from me, and you succeeded – but! your success is empty, you have gained nothing.' And in 1920: 'You have been a lazy, ignorant, bad-tempered arguing troubling making female all your life. ... I haven't one good thought or memory of you.'

They were never divorced (Hattie was a Catholic), but Fields, as a star, had a number of discreet alliances, the only overt one being the last, with Carlotta Monti, an aspiring actress and singer, who saw him through to the end. All the bitterness was turned into comedy, as the clown laboured feverishly to construct the masks which sought to hide the private man. But the clues run right through the sketches and films.

Fields never lived the small-town life portrayed in *It's the Old Army Game*, *The Potters*, *It's a Gift* and its sound predecessors, the Mack Sennett shorts – *The Dentist*, *The Pharmacist* and *The Barber Shop* (1932–3) – the locale to which he would return in *The Bank Dick* (1940) for its final apotheosis and burial. But he had clearly studied the towns and cities through which he passed in his travelling days. Somewhere along the way the milieu began to jell. Perhaps the kind of town that wouldn't respond to his performances. Perhaps the kind of family he might have missed out on, in the recesses of his private pain. Perhaps the need mercilessly to strip and lampoon the hicks hid a deeper desire for that same normality, harassed as it might be.

In Fields's suburban mode (as opposed to his circus face) there were three models of wives: Alison Skipworth portrayed a female Fields, a rare equal partner, in the car-wrecking episode of the portmanteau film *If I Had a Million* (1932). Elise Cavanna was the bizarre helpmeet in *The Pharmacist* and *The Barber Shop*, all legs and eye shadow, as well as serving as victim in the amazingly lewd tooth-pulling scene in *The Dentist*, her legs wrapped round Fields's back as he

At the breakfast table

jerks her about the room by her tusk. And there was the no holds-barred harpie, portrayed in *The Bank Dick* by Cora Witherspoon and in *It's a Gift* by Kathleen Howard. Here she is, rising to the occasion at the Bissonette breakfast table:

> MRS BISSONETTE: Don't smoke at the table! Don't throw matches around! ... Harold, I want one thing settled. If you get the money from Uncle Bean you are not going to buy an orange ranch with it!
> HAROLD BISSONETTE: Oh, no, no, no ...
> MRS BISSONETTE: Don't try that innocent look with me! We need THINGS in the house, I haven't a STITCH to my back, the children need clothes, and we should have a car.
> HAROLD: Oh yes, a car by all means ...
> MRS BISSONETTE: I don't know where you get the idea you can make money raising oranges when you can't even run a corner grocery store.

Kathleen Howard had a singular background, considering her niche in cinema history. She had been a Canadian singer who performed with the Metropolitan Opera and other opera companies around the world. She had also written for fashion magazines, and was fashion editor of *Harpers Bazaar* in 1928, as well as being President of the magazine publishers' Fashion Group. But like her counterpart with the Marx Brothers, Margaret Dumont, her starlight is refracted to us through strange warps of fate. Certainly her first career stands her in good stead as she moves in for the kill when Harold Bissonette, having heard the eight o'clock whistle blow, rises to leave the breakfast table:

> MRS BISSONETTE: Wait, I'm not through with you. Now I KNOW you've got something on your mind. You're CONSTANTLY doing things behind my back and I know nothing about them till you're in some sort of SCRAPE and I have to get you out. Remember that scheme to revive the celluloid collar a couple of years ago? Well, THAT was going to make us a fortune. WHERE is it? Now you've got an orange ranch on your mind. Well, nothing will come of it ...

Harold sneaks off into another room but his daughter Mildred is there to berate him tearfully for planning to take her away from the people she likes. Jean Rouverol, who played Mildred, in her very first film role, had not a great deal to do in the picture, apart from brushing hairs into Fields's mouth and furthering the plot by means of a few mundane lines. Like Tom Bupp as little Norman Bissonette, she is really an accessory to the act, positioned to place Harold, the modern Micawber, firmly between two fires:

> MRS BISSONETTE: Harold, are you listening to me?
> HAROLD: Oh yes, dear, go on, go on ...
> MRS B: What was the last thing I said?
> HAROLD: Yes, yes, every word of it ...
> MILDRED: I never knew such an ungrateful father ...
> HAROLD (to Mildred): Listen, you all have to realise one thing, THAT I (looks around fearfully and lowers his voice) am the master in this household.
> MRS B: HAROLD!
> HAROLD: Yes, dear?
> MRS B: I don't know why it is that every time I want to talk to you you're off in some other part of the house. (HAROLD tiptoes back into the dining room) I have to SHOUT, SHOUT, SHOUT. No wonder the neighbours know all about our private affairs. (HAROLD begins sneaking downstairs to the main door) I get little enough opportunity as it is to find out what's going on, without you running away as if I have the SMALLPOX or something, every time I open my MOUTH!

What were her dreams, this sad, deflated woman, shackled for life with this impossible man? Like Margaret Dumont, Kathleen Howard managed to extract a real dignity and pathos out of a role constructed for a monster. In hairnet and nightslip, Mrs Bissonette continues to express her pain, in bed, with the clock at 4:30 a.m., to the counterpoint of Harold's routine mumbles:

> MRS B: For twenty years I've struggled to make a home for you and the children ...

HAROLD: Yes, you have ...
MRS B: Slaving day in and day out to make both ends meet.
Sometimes I don't know which way to turn.
HAROLD: Turn over on your right side, dear, sleeping on your
left side's bad for the heart.

We can recognise here the contours of another of Fields's ur-sketches,
the 'bedroom sketch', one of the original *Comic Supplement* acts, as
described by Louise Brooks:

> Every night at the *Follies*, standing in the wings, I would watch
> Bill's 'Bedroom Sketch', with Edna Leedom, and his 'Picnic
> Sketch', with Ray Dooley. The 'Bedroom Sketch' opens in
> darkness. Bill and Edna are asleep in a double bed facing the
> audience. On Bill's side is a night table with a lamp on it; on
> Edna's side is a night table with a telephone on it. The telephone
> rings. Bill turns on the lamp and gets out of bed, sodden with
> sleep, his hair on end, wearing rumpled old white pyjamas. He

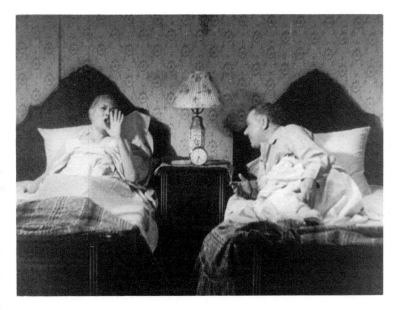

The bedroom sketch

trots round the bed on his little pink feet to answer the telephone. After mumbling a few words, he says, 'Good night, Elmer.' Then, looking down at Edna, who neither moves nor speaks, he adds, 'That was Elmer.'

In the original sketch, Fields's companion, Edna, turned out to be a ravishing blonde, but time has passed. She is now in her ragged, worn-out middle age. The bedside lamp is now beside the clock between the two beds, and the telephone call is not from 'Elmer' but from an anonymous caller asking for the maternity hospital. Mrs Bissonette's suspicions are aroused: 'Funny thing they should call you here at this hour of the night from the maternity hospital.' 'They didn't call me up from the maternity hospital,' mumbles Harold, 'they wanted to know if this was the maternity hospital.' 'Oh, don't make it any worse.' Mrs Bissonette turns over wearily, but Harold's mumbles merely fuel the embers.

> MRS B: I don't know how you expect anybody to get any sleep, hopping in and out of bed all night, tinkering around the house, waking up for telephone calls. You have absolutely no consideration for anybody but yourself. I have to get UP in the morning, get breakfast for YOU and the children, I have no MAID, you know, probably never shall ...

Is there an echo of the call that Fields never received, never could receive, from the maternity hospital, absent as he had been at his only son's birth? Certainly one can hear the cadences of old dead arguments flowing into the litany of woe: the clown's malicious rewrite of old wounds that never healed.

The script gives us few clues as to Mrs Bissonette's past, maiden or otherwise. We might interpolate our own reading of a woman trapped in a world she is terrified of losing. The Depression era fear of loss of earnings and home echoes through her horror-struck opposition to Harold's plans to buy the orange ranch in California. But she shoulders the burdens come what may.

Later, when Harold is transporting the family across country in his loaded jalopy like a clan of uprooted Oakies, she is still trying to uphold a semblance of order. On the way, an important clue emerges. Stopping en route at a camping site, Harold, after a vain tussle with a deckchair, which he eventually throws on the fire, joins a group of men yodelling by the campfire. This is, if one thinks of it, the only visual hint in the film of the kind of landscape created by the Depression, but this bucolic gathering is a far cry from the nomadic workseekers of real-life 1934. The men are singing 'When the moonlight rests tonight upon the Wabash', the same song, interestingly, that the burglars sing in the cellar in *The Man on the Flying Trapeze* (1935), Fields's second bout with Kathleen Howard. Fields offers to join them, with the comment 'In my youth, I used to belong to the Cahauxin Hose Glee Club in Philadelphia', and has just begun a chorus of 'The Two Sweethearts' when Mrs Bissonette, listening appalled from her tent, lets fly with an old boot, knocking his hat off.

Do we glimpse, in the unerring accuracy of this throw, the lost hand of Hattie, the juggler's long-suffering assistant? At any rate, in the picnic scene following, when the Bissonettes lay waste to a rich landowner's private lawn, Mrs Bissonette gives bent to a deeper woe when she vainly tries to stop Harold beating off an attack by his dog with the pillows she has brought from their old home: 'Oh, you idiot! Those were my mother's feathers!' A plaintive cry at a long-lost security, the torn link with a better age?

6
CLOSED ON ACCOUNT OF MOLASSES

Let us return to early morning in Wappinger Falls. Escaping from Mrs Bissonette's breakfast litany, Harold repairs to his place of work. The grocery store scene in *It's a Gift* is Harold's second epic battle with the forces of obstruction. It has all the fury and pathos of Chaplin's struggle against the elements in *The Gold Rush*, only here chaos is represented not by blizzards and starved prospectors but by the mundane citizens of the town. To wit: Everett Ricks – the ubiquitous Tammany Young as Harold Bissonette's dim-witted shop assistant; Jasper Fitschmueller, cumquat-consumer-in-waiting; Mr Muckle, the blind man who destroys everything in his path; and Baby Dunk, the youngest vandal in history.

Although the scene derives from another of Fields's basic sketches, 'The Drug Store' from *The Comic Supplement*, through its development in *It's the Old Army Game* and *The Pharmacist*, it has been completely recast, relocated and transformed by a range of new material. It opens quietly with Fields shooing away a little girl who wants to play hopscotch with him and fiddling with the lock on the door of the store, whose other panel is already open. He walks in to find the irascible Mr Fitschmueller already waiting with the immortal order: 'I want ten pounds of cumquats and I'm in a hurry.'

'Yes, yes, yes, I'll be right with you, half a tick.' Harold rushes into the back room, classically fiddling with his white coat and hat while fussing about with his assistant: 'Don't speak to people with a toothpick in your mouth. Go out and sweep the store.' Then he pauses to contemplate the brochure of his dream purchase: a typical California orange grove. A reverie interrupted by the call of Mr Fitschmueller: 'How about my cumquats?'

'Coming, coming, coming!' With his foot stuck in the waste-

'Cumquats, Cumquats!'

paper basket, Harold lumbers back to the counter. 'I'm in a hurry!' repeats the irate customer. 'Now what was that you wanted?' asks the store owner, fiddling with a wire-attached pen.

'CUMQUATS! CUMQUATS!'

'Ah, oh yes, ten pounds of cumquats.'

We cut to a shot of an elderly blind man making his way across the road. From the counter, Harold sees him approaching through the closed glass door. There follows a moment of panic. Waving his hands, Harold yells out to his assistant:

HAROLD: Open the door for Mister Muckle!
RICKS: Whadya say?
JASPER F: HOW ABOUT MY CUMQUATS?!
HAROLD: Open the door for Mr Muckle, the blind man!

Harold rushes to the door, but Mr Muckle's cane, inevitably, shatters the glass, showering Harold with its shards.

Enter Mr Muckle

Robert Lewis Taylor tells us that Fields's propensity for 'funny' names came from the tricks of the travelling vaudeville circuit. He quotes Fields:

> In every big city there is one surefire laugh, and that lies in hanging some piece of idiocy upon the people of a nearby city or town... It's a fact that some names just sound funny to people's ears. When I was a boy in Philadelphia I made that discovery myself. We had a great time at the expense of our neighbour, Mr Muckle, though he was an estimable gentleman with nothing funny about him except the name.

This principle runs through all Fields's work. Augustus Winterbottom, Mrs Windleschaeffer, Cleopatra Pepperday, Eustace McGargle, Larson E. Whipsnade, Sneed Urn, Cuthbert J. Twillie, Egbert Souse, J. Pinkerton Snoopington, Ogg Ogilby, Cucumonga, Paxhatauney, Lake Shosho Cocomo, Pismo Beach, Lompoc, and so on. Charles Bogle himself was based on a bootlegger whose response to Fields's confession that he had used his name for the movies was that he had never seen them because 'the missus and I don't care for the films. Father Dunlavy says they're immoral.' I don't know about Otis Criblecoblis. Carlotta Monti, Fields's mistress and companion, claims credibly that the funny names derived from his beloved Dickens, from Clarence Barnacle, Horatio Fitzkin, Uriah Heep, Mr Barkis, Thomas Bladerstone *et al*.

The actor behind the funny name in this instance is Charles Sellon, veteran character actor in such films as *Bulldog Drummond* (1929), *Love Among the Millionaires* (1930) and Harold Lloyd's *The Cat's Paw* (1934). He also had a small part in Cecil B. DeMille's silent epic of the cross, *King of Kings* (1927). But here he is part of a quite different calvary.

The spectacular entrance of Mr Muckle racks up the tension in Harold Bissonette's store. Mr Muckle is practically deaf as well as blind, and has to be shouted at through an immense ear trumpet. The baiting of the afflicted might seem an outdated and cruel exercise. But the point of the character is that Mr Muckle is totally indestructible. Harold's attempts to stop Mr Muckle wrecking his store are as effective as trying to stop a forest fire with a water-pistol. The store itself is stocked and designed for disaster. A precarious pile of glass goods in boxes stands in Muckle's way and a display of loose light-bulbs is stacked on a table just at the level of his swinging cane. The wired pen to write down Jasper Fitschmueller's order for cumquats won't stretch to the notepad and the overhead basket to collect goods won't work. To cap it, the barrel marked 'MOLASSES' lies in wait, with its tap conveniently placed at the right height for Baby Dunk's little hand ...

Much is said of the sense of timing of the great comics. But as important as the flow of individual gags is the overall structure of a sequence. The grocery store section of *It's a Gift* runs a full fifteen minutes, about a fifth of the film. The entire sequence is played in medium to medium-long shots, taken at mid-height, with predominating two-shots, those shots in which two characters spark off each other, both action and reaction in frame. Such a long segment played in one location might be dull, but the skill of the director and editor complements the performers in maintaining the flow from scene

'Have you got any chewing gum?'

to scene. It is difficult to understand what the reviewer of the *Literary Digest* meant by speaking of clumsy production. Nor is Louise Brooks fair, in this instance, to talk of the cutting ruining Fields's timing. Film is not the stage. Camera, editing and lighting draw our attention to the essential moves in every scene. The classic structure lies in the way the gags build on each other to push the hero to the edge.

Having trashed half the store on his entrance, Mr Muckle is finally seated by Harold, who retrieves his ear trumpet and shouts into it, 'What can I do for you?'

> MR MUCKLE: Have you got any chewing gum?
> HAROLD: Uh, yes we have. (Shouting into earpiece) YES WE HAVE!
> JASPER F: HOW ABOUT MY CUMQUATS?
> HAROLD: Uh, coming, coming, coming, coming, coming.

He turns, recoils from the sight of the pile of light-bulbs close to Muckle, pleads into his ear trumpet:

> HAROLD: *Please* sit down till I come back.

Rushing to get the gum, back to the counter, pulling off enough wrapping paper to wrap an elephant, fiddling with string, while Mr Muckle gets up and fingers the light-bulbs.

> HAROLD: Sit down, Mr Muckle, sit down Mr Muckle, honey.
> JASPER F: CUMQUATS!!!
> HAROLD: Sit down, Mr Muckle. (MUCKLE handles bulbs) Ah, ah, ah, put it down, Mr Muckle, put it down, honey, put it down, please! (MUCKLE drops bulb, then another one. Begins swinging his cane.)
> JASPER F: I WANT CUMQUATS!!
> HAROLD: Coming, coming ...
> MR MUCKLE: Where's my gum?
> HAROLD: Sit down, Mr Muckle, sit down!

In his panic, Harold drops the gum from the paper but wraps the wad of

paper without noticing it, rushes forward, too late to stop Mr Muckle's
cane swinging into the pile of bulbs.

> HAROLD: SIT DOWN, MR MUCKLE!
> *CRASH! THUD! SMASH!*
> HAROLD (physically pushing Mr Muckle down): Here's your
> chewing gum. Five cents, please.
> MR MUCKLE: I'm not going to lug that. Send it.

Reductio ad absurdum is the key to Fields's gags. But where in other films
he plays anarchically with surreal situations, here surreality is the stuff
of real life, the orneriness of the super-ordinary. Though, never one to
avoid the craziest flourish, he answers Jasper Cumquats Fitschmueller's
fuming query of 'Who is that man? Why did he rate so much attention?'
with: 'House detective over at the Grand Hotel.'

The chewing gum gag is a variation on the old Fields 'Drug
Store' saw of the ridiculous purchase: the man buying the stamp from
the middle of the sheet in *It's the Old Army Game*, reprised in *The
Pharmacist*, and, similarly repeated, the cough drop ordered by
telephone – 'What's that? A box of Smith Brothers cough drops? No,
I'm sorry but we can't split a box. Can't separate the Brothers. Yes, we
can deliver – I'll send our truck right away' (*It's the Old Army Game*).

Having arranged to deliver Muckle's empty package, Harold
pushes the blind man out of the door – whose second panel gets
smashed, of course, by his cane ('Ya got that door closed again!') –
across the street – 'You're all right, go ahead, nothing coming at all.' –
as a fleet of fire engines and police cars, sirens blaring, careen through
at top speed. The blind man's invulnerability is highlighted as Fields
stands, hat in hand, hunched waiting for disaster. Exhausted by the
tension, Fields sags back, collapsing into a dustbin, out of which he has
to shovel himself at Jasper F.'s despairing cry: 'Now will you get me my
cumquats?'

The plot now intervenes, in the shape of a meeting between
Harold's daughter Mildred and her beloved, John Durston, in the street
outside the shop. Durston tells her he's found out that the orange ranch
he sold her father is no good, but Harold doesn't want to hear of it and
won't take the offer of his money back.

Back at the shop, Harold has actually advanced to the stage of starting to write down Jasper F.'s order: 'What was that you wanted? How do you spell it?'

'CUMQUATS! C–U–M–Q–U–A–T–S! QUATS! QUATS!'

Shop assistant Riggs barges into the store on his bicycle, knocking Harold right over the counter. Amid the melee, Mrs Bissonette and little Norman arrive to tell Harold that Uncle Bean has finally passed away. While Jasper continues to fume, Mrs B. pins down Harold in the back room to impart the melancholy news: Uncle Bean choked to death on an orange while attending the Epworth League Picnic.

HAROLD: I didn't know oranges were bad for your health.

MRS B: No, but the excitement.

HAROLD: Oh, the excitement, yes, that'd kill anybody.

Some banter follows about funeral arrangements and what flowers to

Collapsing into a dustbin

send for the wreath, while Jasper fumes on ('How about ten pounds of cumquats?'). John Durston arrives, to try to plead with Harold again about the ranch, while Mrs B. chats with a neighbour, Mrs Dunk, who has ominously deposited her little baby boy Elwood with assistant Riggs while she shops elsewhere. Vicious repartee about the soon-to-be-rich Bissonettes between the identically dressed women, and what Mrs B. can wear to the funeral:

> MRS DUNK: Why don't you go to Schmackendorf's? They specialise in such lovely things (*pause*) for older women.

The plot has now been seamlessly integrated with the gags. Throughout, an iron rule is followed: the plot is always subordinated to the comic business, the gags always illuminate character, and thus character always has priority over plot.

The emerging fact is: Harold Bissonette is only marking time in his grocery store. He may be nominally the boss, but everything in the store, humans or objects, is in conspiracy to aggravate his life. The crowning humiliation, after Jasper F. storms out, cumquatless, comes with the appearance of little Elwood Dunk – Baby LeRoy in the first of his two bouts with Fields in *It's a Gift*. His first act, on entering the store, is to crack the clown on the funny bone with a tin of clams.

> HAROLD: Gerrimout of here! Gerrimout! Gerrimout!

The battles between Baby LeRoy and W. C. Fields are legendary, and the offscreen antics of the clown to stop the child stealing his scenes supplied many apocryphal stories, such as Fields spiking the kid's orange juice with gin. On the other hand it appears that Fields wrote a part for the kid into one of his films for no inherent reason except to emphasise his importance to the studio at a point when his option was due, and that he brought him presents the day after he shot the scene in *The Old-Fashioned Way* where he kicks the child in the behind. A nineteenth-century vaudevillian to the eyeballs, Fields liked to keep his sentimental streak well hidden. The child's full name was LeRoy Overacker, born in 1931. Where is he now? One can imagine a robust man in his early sixties, sipping his bourbon by a poolside in Beverly

Hills and chuckling over blurred memories. If you ever come across this book, Overacker, please write and let me know.

Careening through the store in the goods basket, smearing himself with goo from chocolate unhelpfully supplied by Riggs, Baby Elwood Dunk serves notice on Harold that the worst is yet to come. Despite it all, Mr B. heroically tries to keep his business going, responding cheerfully to Mrs Dunk's query, 'What have you got in the way of steaks?' with 'Nothing in the way of steaks, you can get right to them.' But no sooner has Harold donned his fur coat to get into the freezer, extracted the steaks, shooed Baby Dunk away ('Get blood poison out of here!') and totted up the price of the merchandise with the full weight of his arm on the scales carelessly added, than the final *coup de grâce* is delivered. Held by the helpless hand of Riggs, the child plays with the conveniently placed tap of the large molasses barrel. Black stream of goo oozes. Shocked double-take by Bissonette, berating Riggs, who cries plaintively: 'I told him I wouldn't do it if I was him!'

Enter Mrs Dunk, shock, horror: 'What have you done to my

Enter Baby LeRoy

child? What do you mean by running molasses all over the floor and ruining his shoes? You'll never see me in this store again!'

Harold is left with Riggs, stretching his hands to wring his neck: 'I hate you!' Cut to Fields stepping out of the store, mumbling 'That's the spreadingest stuff I ever saw in my life,' as he hangs up the immortal sign: 'CLOSED ON ACCOUNT OF MOLASSES'.

7
....
'WHAT'S THAT? SPEAK UP, I CAN'T HEAR YA!'

W. C. Fields was 55 when he made *It's a Gift*. He was 51 when he made his first sound film. An astonishing fact in a medium which burned out so many so young. When Buster Keaton was 51 he had already been frozen out of the movies for a decade, having had his greatest successes before the age of 33. Chaplin was at his peak in his mid-thirties. But Fields was living through a second bloom. His first career, as the great

clown juggler, had run its course. His silent movies had not hit the jackpot. Loyal fans like William K. Everson tried to claim great things for *Pool Sharks*, but the voiceless Fields is only fascinating with the hindsight of the later work.

The point about the great silent clowns was their universality. The local sites of Hollywood Boulevard, the San Fernando Valley and the Santa Monica mountains became a familiar landscape of dreams the world over. I remember a distinct and unique *déjà vu* travelling in California towards Los Angeles for the very first time: I knew those hills. The suburban sidewalks and lawns and gardens down which the shadow people sauntered were embedded in memory. Chaplin, Keaton, Harold Lloyd, Harry Langdon, Charlie Chase, Fatty Arbuckle, Ben Turpin, all lived in this parallel universe. It was because of the absence of speech that Hollywood became a part of Europe, of India, of China, and not a small town on the west coast of the United States. But the coming of sound reduced Hollywood back to its local mode. When people talk of the hegemony of American film culture, they talk of the hegemony of the American voice, its cultural dynamic, its inflexion, its particularity. Chaplin held out as long as he could, then even he had to speak. Keaton was for years not allowed to deploy his gravelly tones in other than inferior shorts. Laurel and Hardy could perhaps escape being Americans because their characters remained in a pre-pubertal stage, two grown-up babies in an adult world. But Fields is a quintessentially American voice.

I have said that the Fields persona derived from Micawber, those flowery tones, that mock-gentility culled from all that early English literary reading. But Fields transposed that to his native soil. Just as the elder Dukinfield was a London immigrant in Philadelphia, so does Micawber mutate in Wappinger Falls.

Hollywood takes the world and shakes and stirs it and exports it back in its own syncretic brew. The great comics turn their own distorting mirror both on the real and the desired. The Marx Brothers, concurrently with Fields, turned an immigrant sensibility on all the foibles and pretensions of Abie the Fishmonger from Czechoslovakia who dared to become Roscoe W. Chandler, art collector de luxe. Eddie Cantor, quintessentially Jewish, was another successful immigrant voice. Jimmy Durante was East Coast through and through. Joe E.

Brown was an authentic hick from the sticks, but it was Fields who captured, in his middle-aged ennui, the immoral mores of small-town Middle America, a setting more familiar to us perhaps from more sombre contemporary sources, such as Thornton Wilder's play *Our Town*.

Wilder's play was first performed in 1938, and we might speculate wildly about a visit by the playwright to his local movie theatre in 1935, the year *It's a Gift* was released. A fond thought. For here, in Act One, is Wilder's 'Stage Manager' introducing the locale of the action:

> Here's the Town Hall and the Post Office combined; jail's in the basement.
>
> Bryan once made a speech from these very steps here.
>
> Along here's a row of stores. Hitching posts and horse blocks in front of them... Here's the grocery store and Mr Morgan's drugstore. Most everybody in town manages to look into those two stores once a day ...

Mr Bissonette is surely in residence. But there are omissions in Fields's Town, crucial ones, as detailed by Wilder's Stage Manager:

> Over there is the Congregational Church; across the street's the Presbyterian. Methodist and Unitarian are over there. Baptist is down in the holla' by the river. Catholic Church is over beyond the tracks ...

None of these houses of theological quackery rate as much as a mumble in Fields. Perhaps for obvious reasons: if can we imagine the clown's malicious voice turned on religion, the censor and the studio bosses would have made sure those comments were wiped off the screen. Fields remains nevertheless the voice of the eternal non-conformist, with his dream of an orange ranch Walden and his jaundiced Mark Twain eye on fellow citizens. He maintains, in his Bissonette mode, the facade of respectability while subverting all received values. No wonder that it is his wife, the person closest to him, who sees through the surface to the dangerous anarchist beneath.

The truth is: Harold Bissonette is in cahoots with Mr Muckle to destroy his own shop. As he tells his wife, after her tirade at his spending the only money they'll ever see on his orange ranch, contemplating her continued poverty and the need to spend the rest of her years 'depending on that grocery store for a bare existence': 'I sold the grocery store. I'm now in the orange business.'

Thornton Wilder says of his characters in *Our Town*: 'It is an attempt to find a value above all price for the smallest events in our daily life. I have made the claim as preposterous as possible, for I have set the village against the largest dimensions of time and place... Each individual's assertion to an absolute reality can only be inner, very inner.'

A fair description of Harold Bissonette and the Fields persona in general. All those mumbled asides culled from Ma Dukinfield, the private thoughts leaked into murmurs. In the poker game of life, Fields hugs his cards close to his chest. His larger dreams are implicit in small gestures and tics of pain and loathing: the curl of the lip, the narrowing

Mae West and W. C. Fields in *My Little Chickadee*

of the eyes, the hunched escape, the jerking elbows. Inside the small-town failure, J. P. Morgan struggles to spring out, to realise the American dream. But there is, in truth, no J. P. Morgan in there, no grand industrial mogul, ruthless and dire. Just an old-style romantic. To paraphrase Eliot: between the idea and the reality, between the motion and the act – falls the clown's shadow.

The only direct rival to Fields in the 1930s was probably Mae West, in many ways his female counterpart, with her equally idiosyncratic attacks on the morality of the day. They were of course destined to meet, though when Universal Studios finally teamed them in the cod Western *My Little Chickadee* in 1940 (which Fields wanted to call *Corn With the Wind*), it was more a ploy to combine two stars who were believed past their maximum lustre. As it turned out, each star wrote his and her own dialogue, and seemed to inhabit different parts of the film at different times. Mae West could not deploy her full panoply of pre-Hays Code ribaldry, and Fields stole scenes with shameless abandon ('Is this a game of chance?' – 'Not the way I play it!'). As Flowerbelle Lee and Cuthbert J. Twillie, each pursues quite separate conquests: she to ensure control over her men, he to move on to the next sure-fire scam – hair-oil wells in the East.

Confidence trickster, anarchist, solid citizen, that classically American rogue. The schizoid embrace and subversion of social control that links McGargle to Bissonette. And the dream that somewhere, over the rainbow, over the Rockies, lies Paradise – 'the waving fields of alfalfa' of *The Bank Dick*, above the rich seams of the beefsteak mines. No wonder Mrs Bissonette despairs, tossing and turning in bed, as her groaning inventory of her husband's defects drives him out to try to sleep on the porch.

8

· ·

'DO YOU KNOW A MR CARL LAFONG?'

How far back can we trace a comic idea? The 'porch scene', as we have seen, is another of Fields's perennial numbers, constantly honed, developed and perfected over the years, traced back to that 'based on' material of *The Comic Supplement*, written by J. P. McEvoy with Fields for the flopped tour in 1924. Although the sketches were salvaged by Ziegfeld for his 'Latest Edition' of the Follies of 1925, Fields was not, in that year, the hit of the show. Critics at the time were more impressed by the finale, 'Fine Feathers Make Fine Birds', with 'Ziegfeld's girls bedecked in more than their customary allotment of feathers'. Another noted hit that year was Ethel Shutton singing 'Eddie Be Good' to twenty-four Ziegfeld beauties all made up as Eddie Cantor. But the seed had been sown.

And before that? Ronald Fields reports Fields's sister telling him that their mother used to make strenuous efforts to keep people quiet so that William Claude could have his morning nap. But, Claude revealed to his sister much later, he was always kept awake by Ma's loud admonitions to everyone, from the milkman to the mailman, to keep the noise down because her son was 'home now, he's asleep upstairs'.

Essential comedy has eternal roots. The stage 'Back Porch' turned up, as we have seen, on the screen in *It's the Old Army Game*. But Fields himself was unhappy with that version, as he revealed in a letter to a friend, much later, in 1943:

The back porch set

> That (the porch scene we did in Florida) was awful, but I
> sincerely believe I had nothing to do with it being photographed
> the way it was. Norman McLeod was kind enough to let me do
> my own version of the scene up at the Lasky ranch for Paramount
> and that was really a very fine scene.

It certainly is. In *It's a Gift* the 'porch scene', transformed and rewritten,
becomes one of the cinema's great comedy sequences, and Fields's most
perfectly encapsulated comment on Our Town and all who live therein.
It exemplifies the great strength of the 'golden age of comedy', that
ability to stop the plot, ground all the narrative action and settle down
to the real business of comedy – getting laughs through character, with
nothing but the materials at hand.

The scene lasts eleven minutes, the third and most rigorous of the
clown's battles with the universe in the film. It is framed in the stark
proscenium of the back porches of the Bissonettes' apartment house.
There are three floors, ground, middle and upper, divided into little
boxes by the posts and stairways of the separate landings. Harold is in

At work on the back porch set

the middle box of the middle floor, exiting his back door to try to sleep on the hanging bench beside the stairs. The entire sequence is shot head-on to the porch, with the exception of a few point-of-view shots from above to people in the street below.

Every aspect of this set, and every prop within it, will be used to the full. Nothing is wasted, nothing is in the frame for decorative purpose only. The pots, basins, washing lines, dustbin lids, bottles and slamming doors will all be deployed to devastating effect. There will be no distraction, as was the convention in the earlier shorts, of a tinkling music track of the kind which accompanied Laurel and Hardy's sketches. This was deployed for Fields as well, in his Mack Sennett three-reelers, but here there is only natural sound.

Stretching out gingerly upon the hanging bench, Harold Bissonette, in his pyjamas, has a brief moment of hope. But the bench is attached to a cracked beam, which crashes down, dislodging, for good measure, a tin basin hung on the wall. The first of Mrs Bissonette's intrusions booms out from inside the house: 'Harold! Will you please keep quiet and let me get some sleep!'

Harold settles on the fallen bench. But the milkman, carrying his rattling bottles, clumps up the stairs, depositing bottles, a packet of Corn Flakes and a coconut on the sill of the apartment above. Harold, who doesn't see him, calls down to the ground floor: 'Hey, make a little less noise down there.' The milkman descends, bottles rattling, producing another weary interjection from Harold: 'And a special favour: please stop playing with those sleigh bells.'

The sequence that follows puts the lie to the concept that the director is superfluous in a film such as this, despite Fields's memory of Norman McLeod's non-interference. It goes as follows:

Medium shot: The coconut falls from the sill above onto the top of the stairway.

Close shot: Harold, lying on his bench, starts.

Medium shot: Camera follows the coconut as it falls from stair to stair towards the next landing.

Close shot: Harold starts.

Close shot: Coconut falls one more step.

Close shot: Harold starts, waits ...

Close shot: Coconut falls one further step and stops.

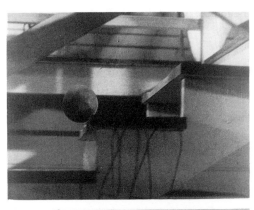

The coconut falls

Close shot: Harold looks up.

Close shot: Coconut falls another step and stops.

Close shot: Harold looks up, then settles back.

Close shot: Coconut falls more steps ...

Close up: ... into dustbin, whose lid flies off.

Medium shot: Cushion flies up from bench as Harold sits bolt upright.

Close shot: Harold moves to place chair under bench, lifting it to replace chain.

This is not just the flow of the performance: it is performance plus camera placement plus cutting. The actor alone cannot convey the effect. This ballet between Fields and the coconut is a clash of titans. There can be no doubt that the coconut has a mind of its own. But there is worse to come: down in the street another nemesis has arrived, in the shape of T. Roy Barnes.

T. Roy Barnes, a handsome and convivial actor, had had his own act on the vaudeville stage, with his wife Bessie Crawford, entitled 'A Package of Smiles'. In silent films he had been a leading man for a while, in films such as *A Kiss in Time, Too Much Wife, Is Matrimony a Failure?, The Old Homestead* and *Reckless Romance.* He was Buster Keaton's partner in *Seven Chances* (1925), but his career declined and he was reduced to character roles. Here he shines for a brief moment of glory, as he strides up the road, his chest puffed out, his fedora and suit bright in the sun, perkier and more bushy-tailed than anyone should be at such an hour:

SALESMAN: Is this 1726 Prill Avenue?

HAROLD: No.

SALESMAN: Is there a Prill Avenue in this neighbourhood?

HAROLD: I don't know.

SALESMAN: Do you know a Mister Carl LaFong? Capital L, small a, capital F, small o, small n, small g. Carl LaFong!

HAROLD: No, I don't know a Mister Carl LaFong, capital L, small a, capital F, small o, small n, small g. And if I did know Carl LaFong, I wouldn't admit it.

SALESMAN: Well, he's a railroad man and he leaves home very early in the morning.

HAROLD: Well, he's a chump.

SALESMAN: I hear he's interested in an annuity policy.

HAROLD: Ah, isn't that wonderful.

SALESMAN: Yes, it is ... (Bounds up the stairs, undeterred by the obstructive drawl.) The public are buying them like hot cakes. All companies are going to discontinue this policy after the 23rd of this month.

HAROLD: That's rather unfortunate. (He has withdrawn beneath his blanket but the salesman stands over him, oozing enthusiasm.)

SALESMAN: Yes, it will be. Say, maybe you would be interested in such a policy!

HAROLD: No, I would not.

SALESMAN: Say, what's your age?

HAROLD: None of your business.

SALESMAN: I'd say you were a man of about fifty.

HAROLD: Ah, you would say that.

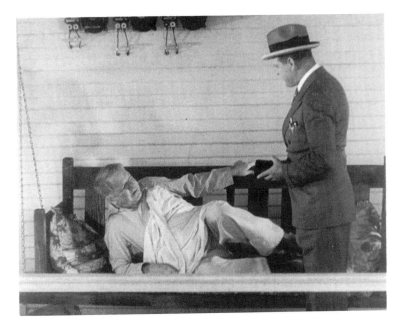

Harold and the salesman

> SALESMAN: Let me see … (thumbing through his notebook) Fifty, fifty, fifty … Here we have it. You can, by paying only five dollars a week, retire when you're 90 on a comfortable income.
> MRS BISSONETTE (entering through door): Harold, if you and your friend wish to exchange ribald stories, please do it downstairs.
> HAROLD: My friend? (Rushes into house.)
> SALESMAN: And should you live to be a hundred …
> Harold Bissonette emerges with raised cleaver. Salesman beats a hasty retreat down the stairs.
> HAROLD (calling after him): I suppose if I live to be 200 I'll get a velocipede.

Another sour exchange with Mrs Bissonette and a bit of business dropping the cleaver on his foot precedes another brief moment of calm, as Harold stretches out on the bench before the next interruption looms, in the shape of Baby LeRoy.

It's worth interrupting ourselves at this point, to examine the porch sequence purely from the writer's point of view. In Billy Wilder's savage satire on Hollywood, *Sunset Boulevard*, the narrator-writer played by William Holden comments wryly that the audience doesn't know that somebody sits down and writes a picture, they think the actors make it up as they go along. In fact, there was so much good screenwriting in Hollywood in the 1930s that we tend to take certain things for granted. Our image of Fields, for example, is almost always of the performer; we seldom picture him hunched over a typewriter, bashing the keys. Such an image might in itself be highly comic, the presumption of Eustace McGargle as author. Nevertheless, it is an obvious aspect of the clown's work throughout his career.

The Marx Brothers did not write their own screen material, although they did write many of their basic routines during their vaudeville period. George S. Kaufman, Morrie Ryskind, Arthur Sheekman, Nat Perrin, S. J. Perelman, Bert Kalmar, Harry Ruby, Irving Brecher and others were the authors of those madcap lines that drove the Brothers' great success. At the other extreme, Chaplin, as soon as he could, took over all his own writing, though in silent days this would be concerned more with structure than dialogue.

Fields, too, hankered to write his own shows, though he was not able to proceed unfettered. He did not script his own silent features and only gradually assumed control of the sound ones.

It's a Gift comes to us, as we noted, through *It's the Old Army Game*, scripted by Tom J. Geraghty. The screenplay writer of the sound film is Jack Cunningham, 'from *The Comic Supplement*' by J. P. McEvoy, based on a story by 'Charles Bogle'. We have established the link of McEvoy and Fields in the original *Comic Supplement* sketches. But can we be sure what derives from 'Charles Bogle' and what from Jack Cunningham?

Fields's 'stories' were twelve to twenty-page extended treatments which related the plot with most of the main dialogue. Screenwriters were then employed to structure the material into a professional script. But the extent to which Fields was involved in this process is also prone to Fieldsian myth. Another Fields scriptwriter, Everett Freeman, who worked on the later 'Charles Bogle' story *You Can't Cheat an Honest Man* (1939), told in an interview how Fields would take the pages he had prepared for the day's work, crumple them up and throw them away, proceeding to ad lib his own version. Fields officially regarded scripts as he did dogs, children, policemen, directors or studio bosses, and he told Carlotta Monti: 'I have no objection to writers preparing my scripts as long as they don't show them to me.' He claimed he could devour a writing team in seven minutes flat, but they were hard to digest because of all those semi-colons and exclamation marks that pricked the lining of his stomach. But if we look soberly at the results on the screen, we might conclude that Fields was too professional a showman to disregard totally his writers' contribution to structure.

Jack Cunningham's other credits suggest a craftsman but hardly the author of great comedy lines: *Shanghaied Love, Jazz Babies, Rider of Death Valley, Flaming Guns, Rustler's Round-Up*. In the silent era he had written top-rank films like *The Covered Wagon* (1923) and *Don Q Son of Zorro* (1925). Later he scripted *Professor Beware* (1938) for Harold Lloyd. He had also written for Fields in *The Old-Fashioned Way*.

I think we can safely assume the sole authorship by Fields of the Carl LaFong dialogue. It has all the Fieldsian fondness for the funny name, lavishly milked for its maximum effect, the interminable spelling made all the funnier because it is unnecessary. If the name had been spelled LaFaungh, for example, there would have been some point in it, but spelled phonetically it serves only to underline the excruciating persecution of Harold Bissonette by the salesman. Carlotta Monti, furthermore, has a revealing anecdote in her book *W. C. Fields and Me* about Fields's reaction to a young insurance salesman who had somehow slipped into his house: 'No one can live forever,' says the salesman to the clown. 'When you grow a little older,' Fields tells him, 'you'll learn that no one wants to.' After the salesman makes the rash riposte that Fields would live longer if he quit drinking, the irate comedian has had enough: 'Fuck you and your company and kindly get the hell off my property!' Q.E.D. Fields was always putting his life into his work.

Fields's penchant for the *reductio ad absurdum* is evident throughout the salesman episode: 'You can, by paying only five dollars a week, retire when you're 90 on a comfortable income.' Fields was always a surreal realist, as evidenced by his earlier authorship of the Mack Sennett shorts, all credited to Fields alone and based on his old routines. The druggist act in *The Pharmacist*, the jokes about cough-drops, the regaling of the browsing customer who finally buys a two cent stamp with a selection of the few books on offer: 'Mother India? Sex Life of the Polyp? The Rover Boys?' Louise Brooks claims that it was producer William LeBaron who steered Fields towards a more real setting for his work, but it was implicit in his original sketches too. Of the early films only *The Fatal Glass of Beer* veers off the reality graph completely, and only his last auteur-work, *Never Give a Sucker an Even Break*, spirals off into never-never land.

We often tend to devalue comedy writing. And analysing comedy is often an inadequate process, taking the clock apart only to find it doesn't tick. The intangibles of the clown's persona, the invisible weight of his or her experience, make all the difference, but without the writing, the dialogue, the lines, the structure, all is lost, as can be demonstrated by the few films Groucho Marx made without the Brothers or their coterie of writers, or Buster Keaton's mercifully forgotten sound shorts.

But take the Salesman–Bissonette dialogue and imagine it in the hands of a modern playwright such as Harold Pinter, or the Samuel Beckett of *Waiting for Godot* (1956):

> VLADIMIR: We could start all over again perhaps.
> ESTRAGON: That should be easy.
> VLADIMIR: It's the start that's difficult.
> ESTRAGON: You can start from anything.
> VLADIMIR: Yes, but you have to decide.
> ESTRAGON: True.
>   (*Silence*)
> VLADIMIR: Help me!

Contrast with 'Charles Bogle' (1934):

> SALESMAN: Maybe you would be interested in such a policy!
> HAROLD: No, I would not.
> SALESMAN: Say, what's your age?
> HAROLD: None of your business.
> SALESMAN: I'd say you were a man of about fifty.
> HAROLD: Ah, you would say that.

Then cue Harold Pinter, taking a random clip from *The Birthday Party* (1958):

> MEG: Is Stanley up yet?
> PETEY: I don't know. Is he?
> MEG: I don't know. I haven't seen him down yet.
> PETEY: Well then, he can't be up.
> MEG: Haven't you seen him come down?
> PETEY: I've only just come in.
> MEG: He must be still asleep.

Try reading the above in the fruity tones of Groucho and Chico. Beckett acknowledged the tit for tat of old vaudeville routines as a key influence on his stage work (consider Laurel and Hardy as the ideal Vladimir and Estragon . . .), and Pinter too revels in that trivial banter which serves to highlight character and satirise social attitudes. Both have found, in the rhythms of ordinary speech, a kind of deeper melancholy, which echoes that of the great clowns. It's clear that both Pinter and Beckett have drunk deep at the same well.

But if it's 'only' pure comedy, is it the lesser art? Ronald Fields, in *W. C. Fields By Himself*, includes a bold absurdist playlet written by Fields in 1922 which, he rightly comments, anticipates Ionesco. Entitled 'What a Night', its cast includes such luminous names as Lord Chava Biggleswade, Bollinger, Lady Sidley-Deasey, Mr Marmaduke Gump and George Bull, a policeman. It features the following kind of exchange:

> BIGGLESWADE: Did you bathe the sun-fish, Bollinger?
> BOLLINGER: Yes, my Lord, they have had their sun-bath.

Further 'non-fictional' essays, like 'Shooting Big Game in Nebraska' and 'Alcohol Has Taken the Place of the Dog as Man's Best Friend, by W. C. (D. T.) Fields', anticipate the marvels of Otis Criblecoblis. And the Marx Brothers' 'Flywheel, Shyster and Flywheel' radio scripts written by Nat Perrin and Arthur Sheekman glitter with a thousand and one sockeroos. Perhaps, after all, one should not elevate the pupils over the masters.

What both Beckett and Pinter lacked, of course, was the lethal asset of Baby LeRoy, whom we see, as we resume the porch sequence, squeezing grapes through a hole in the landing above the supine Bissonette. Harold recoils: 'Right on the proboscis!' He turns over on his back, in time to receive a grape in the mouth, which he spits out into Baby's face. Baby retaliates by pushing a screwdriver through the hole, which sticks into the arm of the bench. Harold jumps up, in time to take another bunch of grapes in the face. 'Shades o' Bacchus!' Running upstairs with screwdriver poised over the child: 'Even a worm will turn.'

At this point Baby's mother, Mrs Dunk, rushes forth to grab the screwdriver and grapes from Harold's hand: 'Not enough you pour molasses all over him, now you have to stuff him with grapes and give him the colic! Come on, darling, I'll give you some ipecac.'

The offended child is taken indoors. Harold tries to settle down on the bench again, but Mrs Dunk's young daughter (or sister?) bounces down the stairs, two by two, upsetting dustbin lids and pans, halting in the street to hold a shouted conversation with Mrs Dunk upstairs (Beckett and Pinter students, please take note again):

MRS DUNK: Don't forget to get the ipecac!

GIRL: I thought you said syrup of squill.

MRS DUNK: I can't hear you, talk louder!

GIRL: I thought you said syrup of squill.

MRS DUNK: All right, syrup of squill. I don't care, get whatever you want.

GIRL: I don't care either, I'll get ipecac if you want to. Where should I go, to Johnson's?

MRS DUNK: Use your own judgment.

GIRL: No, you tell me where to go.

HAROLD: I'd like to tell you both where to go.

MRS DUNK: It's no use, I can't hear a word you say, somebody's shouting on the floor below.

HAROLD: Yeah, it's me.

No sooner has this menace departed than Mrs Bissonette appears again:

MRS B: Who were those women you were talking to?

HAROLD: Mrs Dunk upstairs.

MRS B: Seems to me you're getting awfully familiar with Mrs Dunk upstairs.

HAROLD: They were talking to me, I wasn't talking to them.

Exit Mrs B. back into the house, slamming door. Mr B. slumps back on his bench. But the squeaking washing-line of another neighbour sends him scuttling to look for a mousetrap, poking about for the offending rodent until the neighbour's combinations hit him in the face.

All is obviously lost in so far as any rest is concerned. The last straw is the strawberry vendor, calling out from below. Harold rushes indoors again, emerging with a cocked rifle: 'Vegetable man! Vegetable gentleman.' He lies back, exhausted, on the bench. The rifle falls from his hand and fires, bringing the bench crashing down again with its supporting beam. Harold starts, grabs hold of a fly-swatter, and swats a speck on the floor. Fade out.

Comparing again with the porch scene in *It's the Old Army Game* and in the original stage version, we can see the way the clown hones his material: the overgrown baby in the earlier versions has become the more sinister toddler – the 3-year-old's smile masking his lethal capacities. The humour in the silent version has a crueller, more grand-guignol tinge, as Fields grinds his boot on the child's hand while trying to lift it into its pram. The leisurely build-up and escalation of the interruptions is a vast improvement on the episodic ones in the first versions. Bringing out the rifle to counter the 'vegetable man' is not the last straw in the stage version; it is followed by a long piece with the 'ice man', which *It's a Gift* has dropped. The structure and design of the house is not as well used in the silent film, and, of course, it *is* silent, depriving us of all the mis-hearings of 'sleigh bells' and the washing line/mouse. Vulgar vaudeville, hilarious as it must have been on the stage, has given way to an integrated structure which furthers character, theme and the clown's melancholy outlook on life.

If we go back to Fields's legend, might we not think we are witnessing, in the 'vegetable man' episode, a direct swipe at the vegetable vending father? The overkill of the rifle as a long-awaited hint at revenge against that legendary abuse of his childhood? The

The last straw. . . .

answers lie locked up in the grave. The letters preserved by Fields's grandson provide us with no clue. What we have is the work, to enjoy, to marvel at, and, if we wish, to interpret in its own right.

What the porch scene portrays, so vividly, is nothing less than the cosmic insecurity of Man. Battered by the furies, he seeks in his own mumbled words that 'sweet repose', but everything conspires against him. Human beings and objects alike combine against his modest hopes. And finally, 'Even a worm will turn ...'

Fields was to go on to write five more great scripts, in collaboration with his various screenwriters: *The Man on the Flying Trapeze, You Can't Cheat an Honest Man*, his part of *My Little Chickadee, The Bank Dick* and *Never Give a Sucker an Even Break*. Of these, the freest, most completely Fieldsian structure is undoubtedly in the last two. But it is difficult to argue that, as a single, coherent and self-contained segment, the porch scene in *It's a Gift*, the apotheosis of Fields's oldest, most primal material, was ever bettered elsewhere.

9
. . . .
THE WAVING FIELDS OF ALFALFA

The last section of *It's a Gift* is to some extent an anticlimax, despite its reprise of two more of Fields's vaudeville sketches, the 'picnic scene' and a lesser known skit called 'The Sport Model', written in 1922. To the gramophone tune of 'California, Here We Come' we find the Bissonette family in their car, ready to set out west, loaded down with all their possessions. Mildred says her tearful goodbye to John Durston, and all the neighbours cheer and wave. Mrs Dunk, Baby LeRoy, Mr Muckle and Jasper 'Cumquats' Fitschmueller are all present. After a couple of false starts and some fiddling with the crank, to Mrs Dunk's comment – 'I wouldn't ride across the country with that man for a million dollars' – the Bissonettes are on their way, having somehow acquired a dog which has not been in evidence before.

In the original sketch, included by Ronald Fields in his book of W.C.'s letters and texts, a crazy family – Mr Bimbo, Mrs Bimbo, Baby

Bimbo and young Elmer Bimbo – get in their car for a day's outing. The script says:

> They ultimately get in and get things fastened onto the car, and are all settled, and Mr B. throws the gears into mesh, making unearthly noise. As they all settle in car, rear spring breaks ...
>
> ELMER falls off rear seat of car. BIMBO gets out and beats ELMER.
>
> WOMAN (at second-storey window): I'll bet you would never beat a child of mine that way.
>
> MR BIMBO: You go to hell.

At the end of the sketch:

> Traffic cop blows whistle – Mr B. throws gear into mesh, terrific noise, car falls to stage – the BIMBO family fall out.

Again, Fields lovingly resurrects old material. Back at *It's a Gift*, after detouring across a field to avoid a stalled car, the Bissonettes' first stop is the camping site, where Fields joins in a chorus of yodelling men and his attempted rendition of 'Two Sweethearts' is brought to an abrupt close by a well-aimed boot thrown by Mrs Bissonette. Fade out.

Entering California, they drive on to the grounds of an opulent mansion, oblivious to the 'No Trespassing' signs, careening straight on to the lawn and smashing down a Venus de Milo. Harold: 'She ran out right in front of the car.' The lawn scene is a replica – much more faithful than the other reprises in *It's a Gift* – of Fields's famous 'picnic scene' in *It's the Old Army Game*, though here it is shorter and does not have the family breaking into the house. The Bissonettes litter the grounds with their picnic sandwiches and Fields gets into a fight with the dog, ripping the family pillows and prompting Mrs B.'s terrible, poignant cry: 'You idiot, those were my mother's feathers!'

Little Norman, torn away from throwing empty cans at the fallen Venus, proceeds to switch on the garden sprinklers. 'Maybe its a sun-shower,' offers Harold (shades of Lord Chava Biggleswade's sun-fish?). The lawn ruined, the furious owner and his guards arrive to eject the interlopers, despite Mrs Bissonette's firm stand, as she declares to

The Bissonette family on the road

Harold after they leave:

> MRS BISSONETTE: Why were you standing there like a stone image when those men were insulting me?
> HAROLD: I was just waiting for one of 'em to say something to me.

Having seen the Bissonettes in their domestic setting tearing each other apart, we are now aware of them as a collective menace to the rest of the world. Harold's petty-mindedness is highlighted by his response to Mrs B. urging him to give half his sandwich to his son. Carefully folding the meat filling in half between the slices, Harold hands down a barren sliver.

When the Bissonettes arrive in orange country, they find that the farm Harold has bought is indeed useless. The hard ground is overgrown with stunted bushes, which Harold fingers with the wishful comment, 'Evidently a young orange tree.' The farmhouse is a rotting shack. Mrs Bissonette and Mildred, with little Norman in tow, stomp off in disgust, leaving Harold sitting forlornly in the ruin of his hopes, with the dog.

'Everything goes at once,' he mumbles. For a brief moment the almost fanatical optimism of McGargle/Bissonette is humbled, in what seems to be total defeat. A more traditional pathos and sympathy for the clown is momentarily evoked. But fate intervenes in a *deus ex machina*: the owner of the adjoining ranch drives up to tell Harold that some fellows who want to put up a racetrack next door need his property for a grandstand. 'Hold out for any price,' says the good neighbour, 'you can get it.'

Fortifying himself with his hip flask, Harold holds off the racetrack moguls, while Mrs Bissonette wrings her hands in the background, as he delivers another famous Fields line. When the buyer complains to him, 'You're drunk!' Harold counters, 'Yes, and you're crazy. I'll be sober tomorrow and you'll be crazy the rest of your life.' But the racetrack moguls surrender, paying Harold $44,000 and throwing in the orange ranch of his dreams.

We now mix to the finale of the picture – the dream achieved: 'BISSONETTE'S (PRONOUNCED BISS-O-NAY) BLUEBIRD

ORANGES'. Sitting in a pure white shirt before a table laden with cocktail shakers, and picking an orange from the lush trees by his elbow to squeeze into his drink, Harold finds his 'sweet repose' at last, while Mrs Bissonette, Mildred and her fiancé and little Norman climb into their brand-new car. A great sigh of contentment and a clink of bottles. THE END.

Fields was to reprise this scene, with greater poignancy, at the end of *The Bank Dick*, when, dressed in top hat, elegant cutaway and spats, he is fawned over by his wife and mother-in-law ('Judkins, has Mr Souse had his café rhum a-la-baba?') as he leaves his new mansion through his garden, only to light out after his bartender towards even greener pastures.

....

Harold Bissonette has triumphed against all odds to reach his Eden. But it was not the Land of Promise for his real-life collaborators. Of the three co-stars of *It's a Gift*, only one, Kathleen Howard, had much of a

The racetrack moguls surrender

career in the movies after 1934, almost exclusively in small character parts. After serving once more with Fields in *The Man on the Flying Trapeze*, she appeared with Deanna Durbin in *First Love* (1939), in Howard Hawks's *Ball of Fire* (1942) and in Otto Preminger's *Laura* (1944). Her last role was in Nicholas Ray's *Born to be Bad* in 1950.

Jean Rouverol appeared in a handful of subsequent movies, including a small part in Fields's 1935 *Mississippi*. She had only two credits after 1938 – *So Young So Bad* in 1950 and *The Legend of Lylah Clare* in 1968. Tom Bupp had a few more small child parts in such movies as *San Francisco* (1936) and *Captains Courageous* (1937). His last movie credit was in 1941.

It was, after all, Harold Bissonette's paradise. But Fields had already reached his Eden three years before, in 1931, when he had finally decided to settle in Hollywood to start a completely new phase of his life.

Fields's silent pictures had been shot on Long Island, alternating with his work for the stage, after Ziegfeld, in George White's *Scandals* and then in Earl Carroll's *Vanities*. But Fields, like Bissonette, dreamed of his 'orange ranch' or, like Edgar Souse, of the 'beefsteak mine' that would really make his fortune. Vaudeville was dying, the silent movie was buried. Once in Hollywood, Fields never looked back. Taylor quotes him on leaving New Jersey:

> When I got over the river, I twisted around for a last look at the skyline. I had an idea somehow that I wouldn't see it again. But I felt young, and I knew I was good, and it was a wonderful sunny day. So I drove on towards a very uncertain future, about the same as I had in the past.

That passage might have been written by a 25-year-old, but Fields was over fifty. To believe his own tale, he crossed the country alone, unencumbered by Bissonettes male or female, taking precautions against the thirst that might be expected to strike in the long desert stretches. Legend has him entering the lobby of a luxury Los Angeles hotel, with bellhops bowed down by the weight of his luggage like so many African bearers, rapping his gold-topped cane on the reception desk and demanding the bridal suite.

These were the Depression years, with American prosperity slithering into the pit. The movie studios were struggling to survive. It was not a good moment for silent comedians unless, like Chaplin or Lloyd, they controlled their own companies. Keaton was the most notable casualty, but there were many more who could find work only as supporting actors. Harry Langdon vanished completely. Fields teetered on the edge. He had no easy time getting the kind of work he required, given that his silent pictures had not been great money-spinners and that he was considered yesterday's man. His reputation for aggression had also preceded him. 'He beat Ed Wynn over the head with a billiard cue,' quaked the studio heads, hiding in their offices. But Fields did have friends in town, like director Gregory La Cava and William LeBaron, his producer, who gave him his new lease of life.

LeBaron produced all Fields's subsequent movies for Paramount, as he had produced his first sound short, *The Golf Specialist*, based on his stage act, for RKO. The first Fields part in a sound feature was as a seedy juggling father in *Her Majesty Love* (1931), a period comedy directed by William Dieterle. His first starring role was as the super-athletic President of Klopstokia in *Million Dollar Legs* (1932). Then came the cameo in *If I Had a Million*, the four Mack Sennett shorts, *International House* and *Tillie and Gus* in 1933.

Depression audiences found distraction in the great comics' fantasies, while the dole queues lengthened in the real world. Of Fields's films in this period only one of the shorts, *The Fatal Glass of Beer*, was a box-office failure. Probably the most surreal movie ever made by a major studio, it appears to have been an almost exact replica of a sketch Fields wrote for Earl Carroll's *Vanities* – 'The Stolen Bonds'. The pastiche of the Alaskan prospector, set against the most unconvincing back-projections ever seen, garnered Fields his worst ever notices: 'The worst comedy we have played for any company this season,' wrote J. J. Medford, owner of the Orpheum Theatre in Oxford, North Carolina, 'no story, no acting, and as a whole ... nothing.'

Fields learned his lesson, and it was not until his last two films that he returned to complete and unabashed anarchy. But his upward path could not be checked. A small part in 1933, as Humpty Dumpty in *Alice in Wonderland*, teamed him for the first time with Norman McLeod and brought him back in touch with that band of regular comedy directors – Edward Cline, Eddie Sutherland, Norman Taurog, William Beaudine, Clyde Bruckman and Leo McCarey – those often unsung craftsmen who had worked with Buster Keaton, Laurel and Hardy, the Marx Brothers and Mae West. Without their skill the rhythm and flow of the great clowns, despite their profound fears of directorial dissection, might well have faltered and ground to a halt.

By the mid-1930s Fields was one of Hollywood's top-grossing stars. He could afford to escape public and private worries. But we do not gain the impression, from any of the sources, of a happy man. He lived, during this period, in a succession of houses, the first in Toluca Lake, near Burbank, collecting expensive motor cars, worrying about his neighbours and indulging to the full his worsening vice of strong drink. (The shrewish mother-in-law, Mrs Nesselrode, in *The Man on The Flying Trapeze*: 'I made a vow that lips that had touched alcohol would never touch mine.' 'A very pretty sentiment,' mumbles Fields.)

Taylor makes the excuse for Fields that he never appeared drunk on stage and that liquor quickened his senses, but there is no doubt that Fields was one of show-business's most celebrated boozers. His famous line was: 'I exercise extreme self-control, I never drink anything stronger than gin before breakfast.' But the penalty for years of abuse was not long coming. Various illnesses in 1935 were made critical by the toll of the bottle. He ended up in hospital with pneumonia and was then moved to Las Encinas Sanatorium, suffering classic delirium tremens. He had chronic insomnia, and prowled the grounds of the sanatorium at night, talking to imaginary intruders. Even back in his own house he was paranoid, and would keep his servants awake by having loud conversations with non-existent bodyguards in order to scare off kidnappers and burglars: ' "Are you ready, Joe, Bull, Mugsy?" he'd yell around 2 a.m., "let's go down and get 'em, then. Take it a little easy – I know you boys are former prize fighters and gunmen but I'd rather you didn't shoot to kill. Try to get them in the spinal cord or the pelvis. Ha ha ha ha – this ought to be good!" ' (Taylor, page 215.)

After his bout with the d.t.s, film work became difficult for a while but Fields found a new audience through radio. His gravelly voice, teamed with Edgar Bergen and the dummy Charlie McCarthy in the 'Chase and Sanborn Hour', actually widened his appeal, and it was his radio shows that enabled him to stage a proper return to movies in 1939

P1236-15

Norman Z. McLeod

to make his last great films, for Universal: *You Can't Cheat an Honest Man*, *My Little Chickadee*, *The Bank Dick* and *Never Give a Sucker an Even Break*.

During this period, from 1933, Fields was living with an aspiring actress and singer, Carlotta Monti, whom he met shooting publicity stills for *Million Dollar Legs*. She became his mistress, nurse and keeper and stayed with him to the end of his life. Her book about him, *W. C. Fields and Me* (written with Cy Rice), is a somewhat gushing blend of gossip and anecdotes, including the claim that Fields had a second, illegitimate, son by an old flame in the Ziegfeld chorus, who once came all the way from Newark to see his father and was turned away without meeting him. Miss Monti recounts the battles Fields had with writers, and his ascerbic comment, to an interviewer, on marriage: 'I believe in tying the marriage knot, as long as it's round the woman's neck.'

Fields's relationship with women remains ambivalent. Louise Brooks wrote that he had been scarred by rejections in his vaudeville days which he believed were due to his ugliness and the eczema which was so severe on his nose and hands that he often had to perform with gloves. His biographer, Taylor, claimed that Fields had been put off promiscuous sex in his early twenties after watching a VD saga in an unnamed Midwestern town, with such revelations as 'eighty-two per cent of all white, Protestant males between the heights of five feet two and six feet eight are exposed to syphilis on an average of eleven times a year in public drinking places.' Fields liked to say that this show permanently altered his outlook. Carlotta Monti does quote his nervous jokes on the subject, telling an insistent interviewer that his greatest fear was VD and answering the query, 'Have you ever been exposed to great risk?' with the riposte, 'Yes, sitting on a toilet seat after Greg La Cava just got off.'

The real trauma was different. Ronald Fields provides evidence that W. C. never got over his separation from Hattie and his subsequent rejection by his son. Certainly the virulent letters to his estranged wife rumble down the years, to 1933: 'Dear Hattie, I am in receipt of your complaint number 68427 . . .' Ronald Fields traces the stereotyped sweet young daughters in his grandfather's films to his desire for a daughter he never had, who would, he believed, have seen through Hattie's shrewish wiles. But she remains, as we can see, a fantasy figure, much less palpable than the disobedient little male brats who clutter up the Bissonettish households.

Carlotta Monti, presenting a different Fields altogether, claims that Woody (her obscure nickname for him; he called her the Chinaman, after the oriental robes she liked to wear) was a dream lover who had, before her, changed girl-friends every seven years. It is unlikely that in the power game of Hollywood an ugly but charismatic and successful man such as Fields would be bereft of sexual outlets. But it was Carlotta Monti who provided the companionship that alleviated his deep-seated loneliness.

'I was born lonely,' he once told Gene Fowler, reminiscing on his solitary life on the road in the early days, looking into people's houses to glimpse the family life he had sacrificed for his art. This was the real Fields: the man who could never stop working, never stop planning different angles for his act during a working life which spanned forty-five years. From the outset he had neglected his wife and child for his career, and they enacted upon him a bitter revenge which drove him into his shell, his brooding ground of grouches and grumps.

Fields could never distinguish between private and public grievances. Along with children, dogs, wives, mothers-in-law, bankers, insurance salesmen and vegetable men, he had a raft of other familiar prejudices. Foreigners were weird. Blacks were fair game for mumbled comments like 'There's a Ubangi in the fuel supply', though he once wrote a letter to Hearst, the newspaper magnate, to protest against discrimination. Taylor also tells us that Fields loathed racialism, but his will, which was fiercely contested by Hattie and son Claude, left most of his estate to be used to set up a 'W. C. Fields College for Orphan White Boys and Girls, Where No Religion of Any Sort is to be Preached'. It was originally meant to be a college for coloured children, but, Taylor claims, Fields changed his mind in a fit of pique at the supposed insolence of a black servant. His only politics appeared to be those of all-round apathy. He once said that the world's leaders should be put in a stadium and forced to fight out their differences personally with sackfuls of dung.

Was he an abused child? Did his father really beat him? Which version should we believe, his own carefully cultivated myth or his estranged family's formal memories? We certainly find few echoes of a paternal trauma in the films, though we are awash in nagging wives, mothers-in-law and brats. There is a harsh grandfather in *Sally of the Sawdust* and *Poppy*, which were not written by Fields. But elsewhere Fields himself is the father, long-suffering, generous and cunning in equal proportion, the worm that finally turns. Ever vulnerable, he remained insecure to the end.

On his last day, Christmas Day of 1946, Carlotta Monti tells us, he suddenly said to her, after his long struggle with illness: 'Grab everything and run. The vultures are coming.' And his last words were: 'Goddamn the whole friggin' (?) world and everyone in it but you, Carlotta.'

He remained an atheist to the last. When Gregory La Cava asked him once, 'Why don't you ever give a sucker an even break? Why do you have to squeeze out the last penny?', he answered: 'I will explain my philosophy. Most people have a feeling they are going to be reincarnated and come back to this life. Not me. I know I'm going through here only once.'

Decades after his death, his grandson found a number of scribbled pencilled notes. Some were incomprehensible, others plaintive and poignant: 'I need these characters to work with ... It's my act ... If you take away my tools I'm not me.'

Since his death, Fields's reputation has waxed and waned. Robert Lewis Taylor's biography, published in 1949, rekindled the myth, but during the early 1950s most of the 30s comedies were an old, faded memory. Television screenings and film clubs created new audiences and in the 60s the anarchic humour of the great clowns appeared to prefigure the age of Yippies and acid-heads. The Brothers were the right kind of Marxists, and Fields was 'the little guy who looked life in the eye and told it where to go'. But the real Fields remained hidden.

Today, in a world more attuned to the improprieties of prejudice, Fields's broadsides against all and sundry might make him a less popular rebel. But perhaps Fields is due another revival as the most 'politically incorrect' of all comics. Critics said of him that his appeal was essentially limited to men, whose unspoken gripes he shamelessly uttered. Carlotta Monti once asked director Eddie Sutherland, 'Why isn't Woody the greatest star in the world?', and Eddie answered, 'Because women don't like him.'

But the image of the misanthrope, which Fields so cultivated in his personal life even more than in his film image, is, I believe, misleading. For Fields's career exemplifies the eternal optimist hiding inside the shell of the pessimist. He is the quintessential boy who ran away from home to join the circus. Out of an unpromising and in fact mundane start, he impressed himself upon the world by the sheer force of his stubbornness and his talent. He appears, in every film, to be walking in a minefield. The tics, the grimaces, the gliding escapes from self-inflicted troubles, the absurdly transparent chicanery, the stage clumsiness masking the grace of perfectly controlled movement. It is, as with another gross body, Oliver Hardy, like watching an elephant dance. Once again, one returns to Mr Micawber: ' "And then," said Mr Micawber ... "I have no doubt I shall, please Heaven, begin to be beforehand with the world, and to live in a perfectly new manner, if – in short, if anything turns up." '

Harold Bissonette, stubbornly gazing at his beloved brochure of the 'typical California orange ranch' in the grocery store through which Mr Muckle and Baby LeRoy are rampaging, mutters: 'I got my heart set on a thing, I'm goin' through with it.' And, in the realm of fantasy, his nagging family always comes round in the end. 'You're an old idiot,' says Mrs Bissonette after he's won his orange ranch despite all, 'but I can't help loving you.' 'Give her another drink,' Fields tells his daughter.

The comedy of Fields's work was that despite all odds he triumphed, and benefited those around him who had demonstrated no faith in his star. The tragedy of Fields's life was that, despite his real triumphs, success only fed him more anxiety and he was never free of mistrust and fear. If we love the clown, for all the failings of the man, it is because he transformed that mistrust, that fear of failure and disaster, into those cathartic laughs. Fields's life, his follies, his fortunes, his dreams and nightmares, and every fault line of his demanding, quarrelsome character, were etched into his films, never more revealing perhaps than in that deceptively minor, low-budget venture so aptly titled *It's a Gift*.

It was indeed a gift. But never was the pain of the man so visible on the mask.

CREDITS

It's a Gift

USA
1934
Production company
Paramount Productions Inc.
An Adolph Zukor
Presentation
US premiere
4 January 1935
UK tradeshow
28 December 1934
UK release
22 April 1935 by Paramount
Film Service Ltd.
Producer
William LeBaron
Executive producer
Emmanuel Cohen
Director
Norman McLeod
Screenplay
Jack Cunningham
from a story by Charles
Bogle (i.e. W. C. Fields)
based on a play *The Comic
Supplement* by J. P. McEvoy
[**Contributors to special
sequences**
Eddie Welch, John Sinclair,
Lou Breslow, Harry Ruskin
Contributors to treatment
Garnett Weston, Claude
Binyon, Paul Gerard Smith,
Howard J. Green
(screenwriting team
probably ignored by Fields)]
**Photography
(black and white)**
Henry Sharp
Art directors
Hans Dreier, John B.
Goodman
Sound
Earl S. Hayman
73 minutes
6,009 feet

W. C. Fields
Harold Bissonette
Kathleen Howard
Amelia Bissonette
Jean Rouverol
Mildred Bissonette
Julian Madison
John Durston
Tom Bupp
Norman Bissonette
Baby Le Roy
Baby Elwood Dunk
Tammany Young
Everett Ricks
Morgan Wallace
Jasper Fitschmueller
Charles Sellon
Mr Muckle
Josephine Whittell
Mrs Dunk
T. Roy Barnes
Insurance salesman
Diana Lewis
Miss Dunk
Spencer Charters
Estate guard
Guy Usher
Harry Payne Bosterly
Del Henderson
Clarence Abernathy
Jerry Mandy
Vegetable man
William Tooker
Old man
Edith Kingdon
Old woman
Patsy O'Byrne
Mrs Frobisher
Jane Withers
Hopscotch girl
Jack Mulhall
Butler
**Chill Wills and the
Avalon Boys**
Campfire singers

Bud Fine
Driver
Eddie Baker
Yard attendant
Buster
A dog

**(Roles cut from release
version)**
James Burke
Ice man
Billy Engle
Scissors grinder

(Credits prepared by
Markku Salmi.)

BIBLIOGRAPHY

. . . .

Bordman, Gerald. *American Musical Theatre* (1978).

Brooks, Louise. *Lulu in Hollywood* Introduction reprinted in *Three Films of W. C. Fields* (London: Faber & Faber, 1990).

Deschner, Donald. *The Complete Films of W. C. Fields* (New York: Citadel Press, 1966).

Everson, William K. *The Art of W. C. Fields* (London: Allen & Unwin, 1968).

Fields, Ronald J. *W. C. Fields by Himself, His Intended Autobiography, with Commentary* (London: W. H. Allen, 1986).

Gilbert, Douglas. *American Vaudeville* (1940).

Green, Stanley. *The Great Clowns of Broadway.* (New York: Oxford University Press, 1984).

Jenkins, Henry. *What Made Pistachio Nuts? Early Sound Comedy and the Vaudeville Aesthetic* (New York: Columbia University Press, 1992).

Monti, Carlotta, with Cy Rice. *W. C. Fields and Me* (London: Michael Joseph, 1974).

Taylor, Robert Lewis. *W. C. Fields, His Follies and His Fortunes* (1949. Reprinted, New York: New American Library, 1968).

ALSO PUBLISHED

· ·

L'Atalante Marina Warner
A splendid job of evoking this very special
film's very special atmosphere.
Empire

The Big Heat Colin MacArthur
Recommended.
Sunday Times

Blackmail Tom Ryall
Ryall catches interestingly that moment
when everyone thought talkies were a
passing fad, and digs up some great quotes.
Empire

Boudu Saved from Drowning Richard
Boston

Brief Encounter Richard Dyer

Citizen Kane Laura Mulvey
... Ranks among the best things ever written
about the movie.
Film Review

Double Indemnity Richard Schickel
A fine account of Billy Wilder's struggle to
adapt James M. Cain's hard-boiled novel for
the screen.
Time Out

42nd Street J. Hoberman
A rarity: a book written with enough
enthusiasm to make you want to watch the
film again.
Empire

Greed Jonathan Rosenbaum
[A] brilliantly researched account of the
making of Erich von Stroheim's 1923
masterpiece.
Film Review
A very readable introduction to the film and
its fascinating and complicated history.
Movie Collector

In a Lonely Place Dana Polan
The film is still underrated, and Polan makes
a powerful case for taking it out of its cult
noir slot and installing it as a major classic.
Empire

Olympia Taylor Downing
Downing does a fascinating job,
documenting the problematic production and
showing how the director played off her
personal friendship with Hitler to get it done
at all.
Empire

Rocco and his Brothers Sam Rohdie

The Seventh Seal Melvyn Bragg

Singin' in the Rain Peter Wollen
Fascinating.
Time Out

Stagecoach Edward Buscombe
A hugely entertaining account of the film's
making.
Film Review

Went the Day Well? Penelope Houston
The strength of the best Anglo-Saxon
tradition of film criticism – finely crafted and
intellectually rigorous – is discernible on
each page ...
The Times Saturday Review

Wizard of Oz Salman Rushdie
Witty and vivacious ... shrewd and joyous
... it adds to the movie's wonder, which is
saying a lot.
New Statesman & Society
... his finest piece of writing since his
withdrawal from everyday life.
London Review of Books

**If you would like further information
about future BFI Film Classics or about
other books on film, media and popular
culture from BFI Publishing, please write
to:**

**BFI Film Classics
British Film Institute
21 Stephen Street
London
W1P 1PL**